FOREWORD TO THE FIRST EDITION

CARLYLE, in his biography of Frederick the Great, says: 'Happy the people whose annals are blank in history books'. Whilst the inhabitants of Ardnamurchan have a reputation for happiness and sharing it with all who come, I do not think that the publication of these annals to fill in what has been fairly blank up to now will bring unhappiness to anyone who lives in the Parish. In fact, I believe that this booklet will make many people happy, both here and beyond these parts, containing as it does such a wealth of information within its pages.

The idea for the booklet was first broached at the end of 1980 when a committee, under the chairmanship of Mr G MacMillan, was formed in Ardnamurchan Parish Church to plan how to celebrate the 150th anniversary of the opening of the church in 1831. Amongst the suggestions put forward was that a small booklet be produced outlining the history of the parish from 1831, and to this end a sub-committee was set up with Mr M Macmillan as convenor. The main load of the work of writing up the history was to fall on the shoulders of two ladies – Mrs Catriona MacMillan and Mrs Ursula Hodgkinson.

They soon found that, as in real life, the church and the world around it – social, political and physical – all exchange influences one upon the other and become so entangled that one often cannot separate one from the other. And so the booklet grew to include the beginnings of history on the peninsula, the men and women who left their marks on the place through the ages, some of the folklore and legends that abound in the area, and notes on the man-made monuments and the natural features as well as a record of what the Church in the wider use of the term was doing.

The ladies tackled their unenviable task with enthusiasm and hard work, and deserved our gratitude and congratulations. Inevitably, time caught up with them and prevented them from doing as complete a work as they would have wished. However, we are more than pleased with their efforts and congratulate them on what they have done. The committee envisages the first edition will be sold out quickly and so they would be grateful for any comment, correction or additional material that could be included in the next edition.

VICTOR CRAWFORD

[iii]

FOREWORD TO THE FIRST EDITION REPRINT

Since the publication of the first edition of *Ardnamurchan – Annals of the Parish* we have received many complimentary remarks about it as well as suggestions as to how it might be improved and how other interpretations could be put on some of the contents. We had hoped that this reprint would be an enlarged and revised one, incorporating some of the changes suggested, but a quick sell out of the first edition and a demand for further copies has compelled us to reprint. We still would appreciate more comments and suggestions for a future enlarged and revised edition – preferably in writing to the Editor, *Ardnamurchan – Annals of the Parish*, c/o The Post Office, Kilchoan, Argyll, PH36.

ardnamurchan

annals of the parish

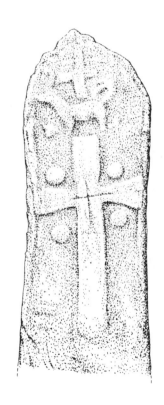

First Edition 1981
Reprinted 1981
Second Edition 1990

Typesetting and origination by Ace Phototypes.
Printed by Summerhall Press, Edinburgh.
Produced by the Parish of Ardnamurchan
with the financial assistance of General Accident **GA**

ISBN NO 0-9515895-0-4

FOREWORD TO THE SECOND EDITION

In the foreword to the first edition reprint the wish was expressed that an enlarged and revised version of the *Annals* could be produced. That wish has now been fulfilled.

Not only has the text been amended and updated where required but substantial sections have been re-written and new material added in order to give a more complete picture of the religious and social life of the parish.

In preparing this fuller version the working group does not presume, however, that it has produced the last word on the matter. In the process of revision it became abundantly clear that there was so much more that could be said – particularly about places and people whose social history is not so much contained in written documents but in the memories of people who are still alive today.

It is the wish of the working group, therefore, that the gathering of material relating to the parish will continue; and it is its hope that this additional material will be published in a series of smaller monographs in the near future.

I am grateful to the other members of the group not only for the time they have given but also for their enthusiastic commitment to the work. If the *Annals* gives as much pleasure to the reader as our preparation of it has given to us, then we will be well satisfied.

It is obvious, from the list of acknowledgements, that many people have contributed to this second edition and we thank them all for their generosity . . . 'if we have seen further it is only because we have stood on the shoulders of those who have gone before . . .'

TOM MOFFAT

Members of the Working Group

Geoffrey Borwick
Catriona MacMillan
Eilidh MacPhail
Tom Moffat

ACKNOWLEDGEMENTS

THE members of the working group acknowledge with thanks their indebtedness to the following for their help in compiling either the 1st or 2nd edition, and in many cases both, of *Ardnamurchan – Annals of the Parish*.

Mrs B Kellas for line and wash drawings and for the cover design.
Mr Alasdair MacLean for permission to reproduce the poems on pages 26, 38 and 58 and for comments on the first edition.
Mrs K Macgregor for the illustrations on pages 57 and 58 and for contributing to the section on geology.
Mrs Marion Little for the drawing of Ardnamurchan church on page 21.
Mr Roddy MacLeod for advice, and for material contributed.
Mr Michael Macgregor for much of the article on wildlife.
Miss Nancy MacPhail and Miss Mary Adam for information about Glenborrodale School.
Mr A Perkins, Northern Lighthouse Board, and Messrs J Clarke and Duncan MacDiarmid for information about Ardnamurchan lighthouse.
Miss Joan Mackenzie for information about Kilmory.
Mr and Mrs John Dye for the map in the first edition.
Miss Helen Andrew for the verse on page 26.
Rev. A Douglas Lamb for early ecclesiastical information.
Mr Rennie McOwan for information about Alistair MacColla.
Prof. Donald Duff, Edinburgh, for much of the section on geology.
Lt-Col B. N. Reckitt for updated information about Sanna.
Miss J.M. Leverton, The Boots Company, for information about Boots operations on Ardnamurchan.
Mr Alistair Garvie, Curator, Mull and Iona Museum, for information about the Spanish Galleon and the 1745 Rising.
Mr Jeff Watson, Nature Conservancy Council, for information about wildlife.
Mr John Cameron for information about the crofting system.
Mr Geoff Robson, Highland Regional Council, for information about population figures.
Rev. Professor J Douglas MacMillan for the section on the Free Church.
Mr Neil Macmillan, for freely giving his personal expertise in the cartography and the facilities of his firm for the typesetting, and for his helpful advice and comments throughout the editorial and printing stages.

And all those who by comment, anecdote and suggestion have added their contribution to these pages.

CONTENTS

Acknowledgements   vi

1. AN OUTLINE HISTORY   1

2. THE MINISTRY AND THE CHURCHES   17

   The Roman Catholic Church   24

   The Free Church   24

3. PEOPLE, PLACES AND FACTS   26

   Crofting and the Highland Clearances   26

   Vikings and others before and since   30

   Mingary Pier and its Origins   32

   Alasdair MacMhaighstir Alasdair   35

   Charles Dunnel Rudd of Glenborrodale Castle   37

   Sanna   38

   Achosnich   41

   Portuairk   43

   Kilmory   44

   The Pulpit Classroom, Glenborrodale   46

   Dorlin and Shielfoot Estates   47

   Camus-Nan-Geall   48

   Ormsaigbeg   49

   Caisteal Dubh Nan Cliar   50

   Castle Tioram   50

   Ardnamurchan Lighthouse   50

   Population   53

   Geology   55

   Wildlife   56

4. ORIGINS OF SOME OF THE GAELIC PLACE-NAMES
   OF THE PENINSULA   59

In addition to the illustrations in the text there is a double page map of
Ardnamurchan and the surrounding area on the inside back cover.

I

AN OUTLINE HISTORY

THE peninsula of Ardnamurchan is the most westerly land-mass of the British mainland. The ancient poetical name of the area is Rioghachd na Sorcha, the kingdom of Sorcha or the kingdom of light. That name may have been coined by bardic licence and used exclusively for bardic purposes.

The present name, Ardnamurchan, has always presented problems for etymologists. Earliest information comes from St Columba's historian, Adamnan, who describes the saint's journey 'per asperam et saxosam regionem quae dicitur Ardamuirchol'.

Other early forms were Ard-na-murrichin (heights of the mariners) and Ardnamurquhac and Ardnamurquan, found in references in 1494 and 1519 respectively.

The Reverend Alexander Campbell, compiler of the Second Statistical Account of the Parish of Ardnamurchan, writes: 'It signifies, in the Gaelic language, "point of the great seas" appositely to its prominent situation amid the larger Hebrides which, with the peninsula, apparently divide the ocean into several seas'.

The 1891 Ordnance Gazeteer of Scotland translates it as 'height of the great headland' (Ard nam Mor Chinn).

From earliest times the peninsula has been the dividing line between the northern Hebrides (the Nordereys) and the southern Hebrides (the Sudereys). It was a noted landmark and danger spot for shipping in the days of sail. The Ordnance Gazeteer refers to it as 'an area more terrible to mariners than any other headland between Cape Wrath and the Mull of Kintyre. A dreary spot in a creek contains the graves of ship-wrecked seamen. The coast line from Ardnamurchan Point to Loch Hourn has long been known as Na Garbh Criochan – the rough boundaries'.

Centuries of change and development, often against a background of strife, are recorded in the peninsula's place-names, in the many legends and historical associations and, more recently, by ruined crofts and moss-covered walls delineating former occupancies.

Kilchoan is derived from the Gaelic Cill Chomhghain, meaning Comgan's cell or church – that is, a place of retreat or worship.

Comgan is the English rendering of Comhghan, which is pronounced roughly as Koe-an, and it is that Gaelic pronunciation of the saint's name which has given the contemporary English spelling Kilchoan.

The abbot Comgan was the son of a Leinster prince and is said to have come from Ireland with Kentigern and Fillan and to have lived in the late seventh and early eighth centuries, eventually settling near Lochalsh in Ross-shire. His wooden image, known as the Coan, was an object of superstitious veneration in the West Highlands though at the beginning of the 17th century it was taken to the Market Cross at Edinburgh and burned there. St Comgan's Day is 13 October.

Saint Columba – known as Colum Cille or Columba of the church because of his regular attendance at services – was born in Ireland in 521 and died on Iona in 597. After instruction for the monastic life at Moville, a monastery established by St Finnan, he began his journeying from Ireland in 563. He visited Kintyre and later landed on Iona, using it as a base for his missions.

It is believed that the gifted missionary and his friends paid several visits to Ardnamurchan, traversing it from end to end. Tradition associates a spring at Ardslignish with one of those visits, and Columba is thought to have rested there. It is still known as St Columba's Well (Tobar Chalum Chille). An island at Port na Cairidh, near the lighthouse, is called Eilean Chaluim Chille (St Columba's Isle).

A ridge high on the hill separating Ockle from Gortenfearn is called Suidhe Fhionan (St Finnan's Seat). From there it is possible to see the island in Loch Shiel on which Finnan founded a church.

The peninsula was almost certainly peopled by a branch of Ancient Britons or Picts. In the sixth century there was an influx of Scots from Ireland and Ardnamurchan was occupied by the Dalriads. They were Scots who came from Ireland and colonised Dalriada, which later became known as Earra-Gaidheal, or Argyll.

Adamnan writes that 'the Irish immigrants had the freedom of Ardnamurchan'. Their language was Celtic from which have come the modern dialects of Scots and Irish Gaelic.

Dalriadic influence is recalled in Suidhe Mhic Dhiarmid between Fascadale and Kilchoan. Diarmid died in about 550 AD.

About that time the spread of Gaelic influence and culture, coupled with that of the Christian faith brought by the Scots, began to lead towards the merging of Picts and Gaels, eventually under Kenneth MacAlpin who became king of the Dalriada Scots in 843 AD.

Towards the end of the eighth century Vikings arrived from Denmark (Fionnghaill, the fair strangers), and from Norway (Dubhghaill, the dark strangers). Raiders became invaders and eventually settlers. They conquered Shetland, Orkney, the Hebrides and the mainland of Argyll, colonising those areas from Norway. That led to everything as far south as the Isle of Man becoming part of the Norse Kingdom of the Isles under Godred Crobhan in 1079. In that year the Scottish Crown was compelled to recognise the Norsemen as sovereigns of all the islands of west Scotland except those in the Firth of Clyde.

Norse influence spanned more than four centuries, so it is not surprising that signs of that influence exist still in place and personal names and in a large number of loan-words which have developed from the Norse into Gaelic. Many Highland clans trace their ancestry to Norse origins, and names such as Acarsaid and the suffixes dale, vat, vik, and ness are all from the Norse.

Its relatively remote situation kept Ardnamurchan reasonably peaceful until the beginning of the 9th century when the way of life began to change as Norwegian Vikings found their way to the Scottish mainland.

One of those on whom there is early information was Ketill Flatnefr (the flat-nosed) of Raumsal, and history links him with Ardnamurchan.

He is thought to have visited the Scottish coast periodically, spending his winters in Raumsal, but when Harald Haarfager became master of all Norway in 888, Ketill and his followers decided to quit their native land. Some went to Iceland, but Ketill settled in Scotland with his family.

Ketill was named Caithil Fin by the Hebrideans. He died in the west of Scotland and the stone circle, Greadeal Fhinn, at Ormsaigmor, Kilchoan, may be his resting place or that of some other Norseman.

Early in the 12th century, a leader destined to become one of the great names in Scottish history was living in Morvern. Somerled, of mixed Scots and Norse blood, was appointed leader by the men of Morvern and with them defeated the Norwegian settlers who lived there and in the surrounding districts. Amongst the Norwegian chiefs killed was Borrodill, reputed to have been seven feet tall; it is possible that Glenborrodale takes its name from him.

Somerled had many more successes and became one of the most powerful men in the area, eventually assuming the title King of the Isles. In 1140 he married Ragnhildis, daughter of Olaf the Red, king of the Sudereys and Man.

A treaty in 1156 ended the warring against the Norwegians and gave Somerled all the lands south of Ardnamurchan. The peninsula itself, though, and all the islands north of it, remained under Norwegian control for another hundred years.

Somerled was killed at Renfrew in 1164 while fighing against King Malcolm IV of Scotland. His grandson Donald gave his name to the clan Donald or Macdonald, who became Lords of the Isles, (Prince Charles being the present holder of that title). Donald's own son became Angus Mor, Earl of Isla.

A story from the period explains the origin of some of Ardnamurchan's place names. It is set in 1266 when, though Norwegian power was waning, the peninsula remained under the rule of a licentious and tyrannical Norwegian chief, Muchdragon MacRi Lochlunn. One of his vassals, Evan Cleireach (Evan the clerk) lived at the foot of Ben Hiant and was warned that his chief was about to visit him.

Fearful for the safety of his wife Evan assembled his family in a boat at Coire-Mhuilinn and, armed only with his tuaghairm or battleaxe, met Muchdragon on a path over a hillock on the north side of Ben Hiant. Evan flung his axe into the skull of the Norseman and fled up a gully to the summit of Ben Hiant, pursued by Muchdragon's men. They grasped his long garment but the material gave way and the story tells that the pursuers fell backwards to the foot of the hill. Evan escaped to the shore and he and his family sailed in search of help on Isla.

The gully up which Evan ran is still called Glac na Toiridh, the hollow of the race or pursuit, and the hillock itself Beinn-na-H-Urchrach, the hill of the cast or throw. The cairn erected on the spot where the Norseman was slain is known as Carn Muchdragon and remains identifiable. The cove in which Evan had concealed his boat is now called Sgeir nan Eun.

When Evan told his story in Isla, the local chief, Angus Mor, (Somerled's great-grandson) sent his son John, called Sprangaich, or the Bold, to take possession of Ardnamurchan.

About that time the building of Mingary Castle, which was to be the seat and stronghold of the MacIains of Ardnamurchan, began, though exact dates for its construction are unknown.

Evidence suggests 13th century origins for the main walls, such dating allowing the possibility of some Norwegian influence. It has been suggested that the castle stands on the site of a fort built earlier for a

Norse ruler of the district.

The strategic importance of the castle site is obvious. Though no longer apparent, there was almost certainly a form of drawbridge and the three great sandstone supports under the entrance survive from the original building. Slots which possibly held the drawbridge chains may be seen on each side of the entrance arch and they too are of the original, or at least the very early, period of the castle's history. The type and colour of the coarse-grained sandstone suggest a Lochaline origin. East of the castle are limestone outcrops showing signs of quarrying work which may have been the source of the lime used in the building. Similarities between Mingary and Castle Tioram in Moidart suggest that the two are contemporary.

Mingary Castle

By the time of Muchdragon's death the Norwegian crown had conceded its rights in the Western Isles to the Crown of Scotland. In 1284, after his son John Sprangaich had cleared the remaining Norwegian settlers from Ardnamurchan, Angus Mor had enough influence to win a Royal Charter grant of Ardnamurchan which he passed to John.

So began the line of the MacIains of Ardnamurchan. John's descendants under the clan name of MacIain retained the grant into the 17th century and the name dominates Ardnamurchan history.

In 1344 David II renewed the Grant of Ardnamurchan in favour of Angus, son of John Sprangaich. The MacIains continued to support their overlords, the Lords of the Isles, specifically through Angus's successor Alexander who joined the campaign which led to the battle of Harlaw, and his grandson John who led his men in a major contribution to victory at the battle of Inverlochy in the campaign to free Alexander, Lord of the Isles, from imprisonment by the Crown.

Links between the two lines were strengthened by the marriages of the two daughters of John's son, Alexander MacIain of Ardnamurchan. The elder, Fynvola, married Hugh of Sleat, brother of the Lord of the Isles, and the younger, Florence, married Alan of Clanranald.

Though remote, the area was not without contact with far-off regions. In 1462 the then Lord of the Isles, yet another John, formed an alliance with Edward IV of England, under the Treaty of Westminster-Ardtornish.

Opposing his father's views however, his natural son Angus Og declared war on both the king and on his own father.

There followed many local feuds throughout the islands and the Scottish Crown found it difficult territory to control, sending three successive expeditions against Angus. All failed, the last resulting in the battle of Bloody Bay, on the northwest coast of the Isle of Mull and due south of Kilchoan, in 1482. In that battle, Angus and his forces comprehensively defeated those of his father and his lieutenants, MacLean of Duart and MacLean of Ardgour.

Mingary Castle was almost certainly the rallying point for Angus and his supporters before Bloody Bay was fought.

Angus was assassinated by his Irish harper in 1490 at Ormsaigbeg and that brought a change of policy by the MacIains towards the Crown. Angus had been a great leader as overlord but now the chief of the MacIains, John, recognised the weakened power of the Lords of the Isles following losses during the recent struggles. He decided to become a direct vassal of the Crown and allied himself unconditionally with the king.

MacIain owned lands in Isla, Jura and Mull and disputed the possession of Sunart with Allan MacRuairi of Moidart who claimed it as a tenant of John Cattanach of Isla. MacIain seems always to have held high rank among the vassals in the isles and had married a daughter of Argyll.

When James IV visited the West Highlands in 1493 he came to

Mingary Castle on 25 October and received the personal submissions of several chiefs. James had a great flair for languages, being able to converse fluently in Spanish, Flemish, Italian, English, Latin and Gaelic.

Not all the declarations of loyalty were lasting and in the very next year John of Isla rebelled. With four of his sons he was captured by John MacIain and taken to the king in Edinburgh where they were tried and executed.

James IV visited Mingary Castle again on 18 May 1495 and several chiefs again made their submissions.

MacIain's loyalty was rewarded when James IV gave him a direct Crown Charter for his lands. From then John MacIain's royal favour and power increased greatly and he subsequently became hated by other islanders.

The death at Flodden in 1513 of James IV reduced state power since his heir was a child. The clans of the west resumed their feuds and revolts. Disputes arose between MacIain of Ardnamurchan and Sir Donald Macdonald of Lochalsh who was then attempting to claim the Lordship of the Isles. Mingary Castle was besieged by Macdonald's forces in 1515 and again, with more success, in 1517. Forcing MacIain to flee, Macdonald ravaged the whole territory and seized the castle which he held for a time, destroying it before leaving.

In 1519 Macdonald, aided by Alexander of Isla, made yet another attack on Ardnamurchan. The recently-razed castle being presumably untenable, MacIain met them at Craig-an-Airgid, just east of the Sanna road and about three miles from Kilchoan.

The result was devasting for the MacIains, John and two of his sons being killed. The sites which legend specifies as their graves are identifiable on a cnoc on the south-west side of Craig-an-Airgid, near the old march dyke between Kilchoan and Glendrian farm. The many followers who fell with them are buried a little further south.

The death of John initiated a waning of the fortunes of the MacIains. His surviving son, Alexander, died childless and in 1540 his last child, Mariot or Mariada, resigned the Ardnamurchan lands in favour of Archibald, 4th Earl of Argyll. Though her feudal title to the lands was sound her people could not accept a female chief, seeking instead a male at their head who could inspire confidence in his leadership.

The clan therefore recognised as leader the active and able

commander Alasdair, Mariot's cousin. He, though, had changed sides, atttaching himself to Sir Donald Macdonald of Lochalsh, and being named on Sir Donald's list of Barons and Councils of the Isles. Those listed had been charged with treason and their lands were at risk of confiscation by the Crown. Under those circumstances Mariot placed herself under the protection of a powerful superior, voluntarily resigning her lands on the understanding that Argyll would re-grant them later. His condition was that the people of Ardnamurchan should promise to give service to him in peace and war.

The records include no further mention of Alasdair. In 1588 his son John resided at Mingary Castle as Chief. He was presumably not young as he asked for the hand of the widowed mother of Lachlan MacLean of Dowart (nowadays called Duart).

Hopes of a re-grant of the lands may have persuaded MacIain that that was a sensible step, as the lady was a daughter of the then Earl of Argyll. MacLean at first opposed the match as MacIain was allied to Macdonald of Isla with whom MacLean was feuding. He eventually agreed, perhaps in hope of winning MacIain's support against Macdonald, and the wedding took place at Torlusk, or Torloisk, on Mull, in one of MacLean's houses.

On the wedding night, when the couple had retired, some of the bridegroom's followers settled in a nearby barn for the night though several continued the festivities indoors with their hosts. One account of subsequent events describes a quarrel arising from suggestions that MacIain intended to remain loyal to his clan's ties. In the consequent skirmish most of MacIain's followers, almost a score including those indoors and afterwards, those in the barn, were slain by the MacLeans.

Breaking into the bridal room they would have made MacIain another victim but for the pleas of his new wife. Even so, he was imprisoned with his two surviving followers for over a year at Duart Castle.

Another version of the event is based on MacIain's own recorded complaint and suggests that the attack was premeditated.

In the autumn of the same year, 1588, one of the vessels of the Spanish Armada was driven by a storm into what is now Tobermory Bay, though the township which has since grown round the bay did not then exist. Though generally known as the Florida, that name was given to the galleon by English interests only after her arrival at Tobermory. Her original name was Santa Maria della Grazia y San Giovanni Battista and for various reasons she enjoyed about a dozen different names during her life.

Several stories exist to explain her fate though all that has been established with certainty is that she was blown up. Her background, and the manner in which she – originally from what is now Yugoslavia – came to be part of the Armada – is a fascinating tale though inappropriate here.

MacLean promised to arrange for provisions and repairs to the vessel if the Spaniards would help him plunder the area, including the islands of Rhum, Eigg, Muck and Canna, the last two being possessions of the Clan Iain. He hoped thus to make a pre-emptive strike against those friends of MacIain who had been incensed by the wedding-night massacre and who were planning revenge.

With Spanish assistance he besieged Mingary Castle for three days, though unsuccessfully, the MacIain's aided by Clanranald routing them with heavy losses.

MacLean had had no intention of keeping his promise to provision and repair the vessel. With anachronistic appropriateness, on 5 November 1588 a John Smollett of Dumbarton, or possibly his brother George, went aboard and crept unseen into the powder magazine. Leaving material burning there, he escaped shortly before the ship was torn apart. The writer Tobias Smollett claimed descent from one of the brothers.

Different versions of the tale suggest different agencies behind Smollett's action. Perhaps MacLean himself had been the instigator, though another source suggests that Smollett was working under English orders.

Other suggested possibilities include a sheer accident caused by crew negligence while handling powder; another, without serious substantiating evidence, links Ardnamurchan to the explosion and its aftermath.

Acceptance of the tale requires belief in the suggestion that among those who perished in the explosion was a daughter of the Spanish king, Phillip. He despatched a powerful vessel and crew to avenge his daughter by killing everyone on Mull. But news reached the island in time for the folk to arrange for three witches to conjure up a fierce storm which wrecked the avenging vessel before she could achieve her aim. One of those witches was Ballodhar, or Yellowspot, of Ardnamurchan.

Since the destruction of the Florida many attempts have been made to recover treasure rumoured to have been aboard her. Little has so far surfaced, or at least little has been reported, though a few siege guns were brought up some time ago and are now in Inveraray Castle.

The bay below Mingary Castle is still called Port-nan-Spainteach – Bay of Spaniards – dating from the landing of MacLean's Spanish allies. About that time the castle was strengthened by the reconstruction of the wallhead defences.

John MacIain survived his wedding-day by only a few years and was succeeded by his son, John Og, who was in dispute with his uncle, Donald, over ownership of Sunart.

Donald was heir to John Og in the event of his dying childless, and waylaid and murdered the young man at Faoghail Dhomnuill Chonulliuch, (Donald Macdonald's Ford), near Kentra, in 1596.

Donald did not live long to enjoy his chiefdom, being killed in Morvern by an avenging force of MacIains and Camerons in the same year, and was succeeded as chief by his nephew John. John's time as chief was marked by continuing dispute and struggle, lasting until his death.

In 1612 Archibald, 8th Earl of Argyll, took advantage of the minority of new MacIain chief, Allaster, to appoint an Argyll clansman, Donald, later Sir Donald, Campbell, to administer Mingary Castle and its environs. Campbell behaved obnoxiously to the local people and in 1624 the MacIains, under Allaster, revolted with the intention of winning back control.

Some of them seized an English vessel and took to piracy. Numbering about 100, during 1624 and 1625 they terrorised the whole north-west coast. They were eventually driven ashore in Moidart. Despite attempts to hide in the woodlands most of them were found and killed. Survivors joined themselves to Clan Ranald and the MacIains ceased to exist as a clan in about 1633.

The name recurs however in isolated incidents and in the history of septs or branches, including that of the Macdonald's, victims of the notorious Glencoe massacre.

Occasional claims arise from aspirant descendants. In 1970 an American living in Manila in the Phillipines visited Ardnamurchan. His name was MacKean and he claimed direct descent from the Clan MacIain. In 1980 a lady from Surrey visited Mingary Castle. She too claimed descent from the Clan MacIain through her mother's family.

Sir Donald's possession of Mingary in 1644 coincided with the last record of the Castle in use as a stronghold. In that year, Alasdair

MacColla, son of Coll Ciotach (the left-handed), sailed from Ireland leading 1500 men to join Montrose and the Royalist forces in the Covenant Wars.

Through he contributed only a fragment to the long history of Ardnamurchan, MacColla, who was later knighted and became Sir Alexander Macdonald, has been described as an outstanding Scotsman and arguably the greatest Highland soldier ever. As lieutenant to Montrose his story is told in the shadow of that of Montrose himself but a strong case exists to show that MacColla was the greater leader.

En route from Ireland MacColla captured a ship among whose passengers were three Presbyterian ministers returning to Scotland from spreading the Gospel in Ireland. They were Mr Weir, Mr Hamilton and Mr Watson. Mr Weir was accompanied by his wife and there were other passengers.

MacColla took them prisoner to exchange for his father and two brothers who were prisoners of Argyll. Landing in Ardnamurchan he captured Mingary by piling timbers and thatch from nearby buildings around it and setting fire to them. He based a garrison there to guard the prisoners in conditions worsened by the efforts to rescue them.

For seven weeks Argyll besieged the castle and both food and water became scarce. Crushed rye and rainwater from the bartizans made up their diet. One of the ministers recorded that 'they were destitute of all comfort, save the consolation of religion'.

Mrs Weir was freed on 3 September, and the remainder, except for the ministers, on 23 September. Mr Weir died on 16 October and Mr Watson the following March. Through the efforts of the General Assembly and of the Scottish Parliament, Mr Hamilton was eventually freed on 2 May 1645 in an exchange of prisoners.

It is not known at what date the castle ceased to be occupied though the north part appears to have been habitable in 1838. Late in the 17th century Ardnamurchan passed to the Campbells of Lochnell who erected an internal structure in the castle and slated the roof. The slates later roofed the old mill at the Millburn bridge after the castle became uninhabitable.

In 1706 the estate of Ardnamurchan and Sunart was acquired by Sir Alexander Murray of Stanhope. He planned many improvement schemes most of which were unworkable. One was a system of dead-level canals to be carried along the hillsides though work on them was never begun. Even his more rational ideas for enclosing and reclaiming land were financially disastrous.

He did however open the lead mines in Strontian in 1722 with considerable success, though in his attempts to bring to the surface the treasure from the Spanish wreck in Tobermory Bay he failed to find more than a few small pieces of gold and silver.

Despite his efforts to improve the lot of the local people he was, for reasons which are not clear, unpopular. He complained of attacks on his property and of plots to kill him. He became bankrupt and his estates were sold to Mr Montgomery and immediately re-sold to Mr James Riddell who continued as owner until his son Sir James Riddell succeeded him.

There are records showing that a straw hat factory opened in Strontian for the wives of the lead miners but there is no further information.

There is no doubt that Ardnamurchan played a significant part in the defeat of the Jacobite rising in 1745. Lachlan Campbell had been minister of Ardnamurchan and Eilean Fhianain – his parish included the district of Arisaig – for over eight years. He made no secret of his loyalty to the 'Protestant Succession' established in the 1688 Bill of Rights under which the Catholic Pretender's claim to the throne foundered.

The Jacobites were keen that he should remain unaware of the identity of the man aboard the ship anchored in Loch-nam-Uamh. His suspicions though had been aroused when, on Sunday 28 July, he noted an unusual atmosphere of tense excitement among the Jacobites in his congregation at Kilchoan.

Similar tension was notable on the following Sunday when he preached, in Kilmory, a sermon taken from Paul's First Epistle to Timothy. In emphasising the passage concerning 'kings and all that are in authority', he was propounding a doctrine diametrically opposed to the views of most of his congregation.

One of them afterwards warned him not to preach such sentiments again since by doing so he might put himself and his family in jeopardy. Campbell retorted that he would continue to spread God's word whatever the consequences.

On his return to Kilchoan a conversation with a non-Jacobite parishioner, Anna Cameron, confirmed his suspicions that the Prince was aboard the vessel. 'I preached a sermon in Kilmory today' he told her, 'and the people were like to go mad. I can take my oath upon it that the Pretender is in my parish'.

Anna asked if indeed he would take his oath on it and his reply, 'According to my present conviction I can' broke Anna's reserve. 'God be thanked that you can' she gasped. 'I was under oath to tell nothing until one could swear that he knew the Pretender was in Kinlochmoidart'.

Though everyone was aware of the presence of the French vessel, Du Teillay, the Jacobites had turned aside suspicion by letting it be thought that she was smuggling expensive brandy and was unable to sell her cargo.

'What number are with him?' asked the minister. 'Six and himself, but word has been sent to all the chiefs about' the woman replied.

Campbell had not the resources to send a message himself and needed someone nearby who shared his loyalties. He turned therefore to Donald Campbell of Auchindoun, the Duke of Argyll's factor in Ardnamurchan, who was at Mingary castle. That evening a messenger left the castle to give the news to Donald Campbell of Airds, who in turn notified the Sheriff-Depute of Argyll in Inverary. The warning, grossly exaggerating the strength of the Pretender's immediate support, reached Inveraray at 6pm on Tuesday, 6 August 1745.

The Sheriff-Depute passed it at once to the Lord Justice Clerk and action to combat the Rising was initiated. Thus the 1745 Rising began in a remote West Highland parish and from that same parish began the action to crush it.

In a letter written some five years afterwards Lachlan Campbell recorded verbatim his conversation with Anna. That letter appeared in the Scottish Historical Review, published by Walter Blaikie in 1926.

It is known that the messenger despatched from the Castle crossed Loch Sunart on his way south though it is unclear by which route he went.

He may have crossed directly from the Castle; facilities for mooring a boat alongside the walls are still visible today. Another possibility is that he crossed by ferry, perhaps the old ferry near Glenborrodale, a road to which may still be traced though it now lies in private grounds.

About the middle of the 19th century the estate was transferred from the trustees of Sir James Milles Riddell to Mr James Dalgleish. In 1855 Mr Dalgleish built a mansion house in Glenborrodale.

In 1897 Mr Charles Dunnell Rudd bought the part of Ardnamurchan comprising Acharacle and the land westwards from Salen to Ardnamurchan Point. The part comprising Sunart from Salen to Strontian was purchased by the Department of Agriculture.

Mr Rudd was a wealthy diamond magnate and decided to build

Glenborrodale Castle on the site of Mr Dalgleish's mansion house. Sandstone, an unfortunate choice of material for the setting, was brought by puffer from Annan in Dumfries-shire. The builder was Donald Fletcher from Tobermory on Mull with labour from Skye and local workers. The garage house adjoining is reputed to be about three hundred years old, the oldest building in Glenborrodale.

Until the completion of Glenborrodale Castle Rudd lived at Shielbridge House, a beautiful mansion situated on the banks of the River Shiel, but demolished by later owners as an economy measure shortly after the 1939 war.

The estate was next owned by Sir Kenneth Clark of the Paisley thread manufacturing family. Sir Kenneth made several improvements including the installation of an electricity generating plant at Gorten to provide a supply for Acharacle and Salen in 1928. When the installation began to deteriorate it was taken over by the Hydro-Electric Board.

Sir Kenneth entertained lavishly. His large house parties often included well-known people who came with their yachts to compete in the races of the Western Isles Yacht Club at Tobermory. The visitors included King George V in his ocean-going yacht Britannia. The castle was let at certain times of the year, among the tenants being Sir Thomas Sopwith and Sir Thomas Lipton, wealthy men and enthusiastic sailors.

After Sir Kenneth's death, his only son having no interest in land ownership the estate again came on the market and was bought by Lord Trent in 1936. He was the son of Jesse Boot, the first Lord Trent and founder of the Boots Cash Chemists empire.

During Lord Trent's proprietorship about 40 crofters took advantage of a housing improvement scheme under the 1926 Housing (Rural Workers) Act. This enabled them to obtain grants of £100 if they were unable to complete housing repairs, and a loan for any deficiency was made by the Department of Agriculture. Most of the crofters accepted the generous terms offered and the results have been highly beneficial.

During the Boots ownership, the hill farms of Ardslignish and Glenmore were used by them to investigate diseases and other problems in black-face sheep and Galloway cattle, both of which found life arduous in the annual rainfall of over 100 inches and on the shallow soil. The pedigree Galloways carried the herd suffix 'Sunart' and one Ardnamurchan-bred Galloway bull became Champion at the Ayr Show and was exported to Newfoundland to start the first Galloway herd established there.

In celebration of the coronation of King George VI and Queen Elizabeth Lord Trent had a bonfire lit on the top of Beinn-na-Seilg. Local men took barrels of tar to the top by horse and sledge.

At the same time the Coronation Plantation at Glenborrodale was initiated, many of the trees being planted by guests at the castle. Plaques bearing the names of the planters were placed beside the trees. Though most have since been removed or overgrown, one was found as recently as 1987. The plantation has just been cut down and re-planting is to start shortly.

During the Second World War Ardnamurchan peninsula was a restricted area. The loch was used for the assembly of convoys and local residents were required to carry permits to allow movement into and out of the area.

One Kilchoan resident during that war was a retired Clyde pilot, Duncan Cameron. His family had the Ferry Stores and his sister was married to the then minister, Neil MacDonald. Duncan had been responsible for guiding the Queen Mary out of the Clyde after her completion there.

When her sister-ship, the Queen Elizabeth, was due to sail he was called out of retirement to pilot her too down-river on the grounds that he was the only person capable of doing it.

On the appropriate day he was collected from Kilchoan and taken to Glasgow, but because of the risk of U-boats in the Firth of Clyde the ship could not stop to allow him to disembark and he found himself en route to America.

During that war several aircraft crashed on the peninsula. A Spitfire flew into the side of Beinn-na-Seilg, killing the New Zealand pilot. Fragments of the aircraft are still found in the hillside. An Avro Anson landed intact on the beach at Sanna and a Whitley bomber crash-landed on the crofts there. There was no loss of life in the latter cases.

Following the sinking of a U-boat off the Isle of Coll a German naval officer's body was washed ashore at Port na Cairidh. He was buried in Kilchoan cemetery though some twenty years ago his remains were returned to Germany.

Aircraft accidents were not confined to war-time. In 1989 a light aircraft carrying fish from the islands to Glasgow crashed on Beinn-na-Leathaid again killing the pilot.

Lord Trent made his Glenborrodale Castle home available to staff of various Boots branches as a wartime rest centre and several touching letters are available comparing Ardnamurchan and the war-ravaged cities in other parts of Great Britain.

In 1949 Lord Trent sold the estate, which was broken up. The castle itself with its sawmill and two of the houses were bought by Colonel M.H.B. Ritchie who lived there with his wife during the summer months. The townships on the estate were sold off separately though Mingary was kept by Boots and there they bred Highland cattle.

In 1969 the Ritchies sold Glenborrodale castle to the youngest daughter of Lord Trent; he had died in 1956.

Very soon after Lord Trent's daughter bought the castle it was converted into an hotel and has sinced passed through several hands in that rôle. The present owner is Mr Peter de Savary, the property developer well-known for his sailing interests, who has carried out extensive work on the building to restore its Victorian ambience. Though once a popular centre for visitors and local people the use of the hotel facilities and the associated shoreline is nowadays restricted to hotel residents.

In 1968 Boots sold their remaining land in Ardnamurchan together with their herd of Highland cattle. The purchaser, Mr Michael Thomson, also bought Kilchoan Hotel and rebuilt and extended Mingary House to make an estate house, a feature lacking since the castle at Glenborrodale had been separated from Ardnamurchan estate on the break-up of the estate following Lord Trent's ownership.

Mr Thomson remained proprietor until 1975 when the whole of the land from Glenmore to Kilchoan, including Achateny, became the property of the General Accident Insurance Company which now owns it.

Ben Hiant

2

THE MINISTRY AND THE CHURCHES

IN the year 1624 comes the first account of a minister of the church to Ardnamurchan. He was reputedly a Celtic Catholic and his name was Donald Omey. His church was probably the medieval building which, restored in the 18th century, incorporated parts of the earlier 12th and 13th century church. His residence was probably on Eilean Fhionnan, a beautiful little island in Loch Shiel. His parish was a large one, bounded on the north by South Morar and on the east by the boundary with the parish of Kilmallie. To the south-east and south it was bounded by Ardgour and the north shore of Loch Sunart and to the west it went as far as the sea.

Craven's *Records of Argyll and the Isles* tells of the appointment of Omey by Andrew Boyd, Bishop of Argyll, to the parish of Ardnamurchan and Eilean Fhionnan mainly because he was such a learned and godly man. The Bishop hoped that the adjacent chiefs would respect him thus bringing to an end the bitter feud between the two lands but unfortunately that did not happen.

One Sunday while Omey was preaching, a young man armed with sword, targe and musket strode into the church, handed the minister a letter from the chief of Clanranald and rudely intimated that Donald Omey should leave at once, otherwise it could cost him his life. What decision he took is not recorded but he finally left the Parish in 1629.

Later in 1629 Duncan McCalman was appointed a Protestant minister of Ardnamurchan by Sir Donald Campbell. It is said that when he arrived in the parish his congregation consisted of his own household and the beadle. At that time a favourite pastime was what we know today as putt the stone. Duncan MacCalman joined the local men in this sport and being a well-built, powerful man he soon excelled, gaining their interest and affection and in the course of time filling his church.

MacCalman was excommunicated in 1650 for complicity with MacColla over the imprisonment of the three ministers. Though later restored, he died soon afterwards, in 1672.

Following MacCalman's excommunication Martin McIlvra was admitted to his place in 1650 though he too had been excommunicated in

1648 for 'siding with the rebels'. He had translated the Book of Nehemiah into Gaelic and was officially rebuked in 1658 for taking ten weeks absence from his charge for his private affairs and for 'gross un-Christian claims'. He was eventually deposed from the ministry and stripped of all his goods, to his utter ruin, though later he was given £100. He died in 1687.

From 1687 Alexander MacDonald was minister in Kilchoan and Eilean Fhionnan. Known to his Gaelic-speaking friends as Maighister Alasdair, he was of immense physical strength with an equally great scholarly intellect. He walked from his home at Dalilea the thirty miles to Kilchoan in order to preach there.

He had been ordained into Holy Orders in the Episcopalian Church but after the Settlement was required to become a Presbyterian which he refused to do. He was deposed for non-jurancy in 1697. Despite this, his popularity with his flock was such that he had no difficulty in retaining his charge, his congregation refusing to accept the appointment of his successor.

John McCalman, (thought not to have been a relation of the earlier minister of the same name), was appointed to the Kilchoan parish in 1700. The Kilchoan people, though, kept the doors of their church firmly closed against him despite the arrival of a minister from Morvern in full Highland dress to assist him. The Morvern minister was forced to declare the church vacant and to appoint Mr MacCalman the minister there from outside the building.

During the lifetime of Maighister Alasdair no other minister was established at Kilchoan. Until his death at Dalilea House in 1724 he continued to minister to his Protestant congregation on Eilean Fhionnan and is buried on the island.

John McCalman died, aged 42, in 1701. He had married Elizabeth McArthur who survived him. She received ¼s allowance from the Centisma Fund and lived for some years in great poverty.

James Stevenson was ordained in 1703 and stayed until February 1732, his period in office covering the year of the 1715 Jacobite Rising.

Daniel MacLauchlan had been charged in 1733 with intemperance, profanity, and the singing of indecent songs but the charges were found not proven in August 1734 and he was ordained at Kilchoan the following month. He stayed only until November and was imprisoned in King's Bench Prison, London, in July 1735 on suspicion of being the author of *A Vile, Abominable and Obscene Pamphlet dedicated to a Noble Peer*. The publication was in fact an essay on 'Improving and Adding to the Strength of Great Britain and Ireland by Fornication.'

Minister of Ardnamurchan and Eilean Fhianain from 1737, Lachlan Campbell has been mentioned earlier in connection with the 1745 Rising. After his death in 1756 the Duke of Argyll presented Donald Campbell, the elder son of Neil Campbell and minister of Colonsay and Jura. He died in 1759.

There is no record of a minister being appointed for the next two years and in 1761 Kenneth MacCauley was translated to Kilchoan from Harris. During his ministry the old church on the hill above Kilchoan village was built and the burial ground attached.

The Old Church

The church, a ruined and roofless shell, is now scheduled as an ancient monument. It lies, surrounded by its graveyard, about 400 metres from the present church and, though largely of 18th century construction, incorporates parts of the earlier medieval building. It is a little over 14m long and about 5m wide and a point of interest is the wall thickness, over a metre in places.

The south wall is probably 18th century and contains an entrance doorway and three window openings. A second entrance near the east end of the north wall is also 18th century but is now blocked. Much of the reconstruction in the west gable has incorporated the medieval structure though a splayed window with a blocked daylight opening may be an 18th century replacement of the medieval original window.

In the cemetery a long flat stone with carvings in Celtic design is still in excellent preservation. The local tradition that it was brought from

Iona may well be true, for there is evidence that the Lords of the Isles gave the lands of Grigadale to the monks of Iona.

Mr MacAuley went to Cawdor in 1772. Unusually there were only two ministers present when Angus Fletcher, presented by the Duke of Argyll, was ordained in 1773. He died in 1775 and Patrick McArthur, again presented by the Duke of Argyll, was admitted to the parish in the same year but left in 1779 having exchanged livings with the presentee of Torosay.

Donald Skinner was ordained a missionary at Strontian in 1779. He came to Kilchoan in that year and died in 1787. He had five children, of whom two sons went to Novia Scotia. One was a doctor and the other a lighthouse keeper at Cape Breton.

Presented by John, Duke of Argyll, Alexander Campbell was ordained in Kilchoan in 1788. He compiled and was the author of the First Statistical Account of Ardnamurchan and Sunart. The Session Book records that in 1793 he was paid a one guinea note by the Duke's factor for a piece of timber which 'the sea threw ashore at Kintrea' (now called Kentra).

The note was stopped because the bank, Messrs A.G.A. Thomson of Glasgow, was insolvent. It was retained in the hope that the bank would become solvent again and in 1796 the church received eighteen shillings for it.

Mr Campbell died in 1803 but did not minister to his parish after 1797 for reasons which the Session Book does not record. However, there was present an assistant minister, Donald Campbell (no relation to the previous incumbent of the same name) who ministered to the parish until 1804. Admitted in that year after presentation by John, Duke of Argyll, John Patience had been ordained a missionary at Strontian in 1797. Once more, only two ministers attended his admittance.

At the first meeting of the Session Mr Patience asked for an account of the state of the parish and was told that it was very bad. There were only two elders and no money had been handed to the poor for two years. Furthermore, the Session books had not been handed over and were still in the possession of Mr Donald Campbell. The records show that the Session Clerk was requested to recover them before the next meeting and was able to do so.

Mr Patience died at Kilchoan in 1827, unmarried, and is buried in the old graveyard. His grave originally had four walls and a roof though they are now in ruins.

Angus McLaine was born on Mull about 1799, second son of a branch of the McLaine of Lochbuie family. Presented by George, Duke of Argyll, he was admitted to the parish in 1827. The chief feature of his incumbency was the planning and building of the new church.

The old church on the hill was in a ruinous state and it was decided by a committee to look into the matter of either repairing it and its manse or building new ones.

The committee comprised: Sir James Milles Riddell (proprietor); Ronald George MacDonald, Esq., of Clanranald; Col. Robertson MacDonald of Kinlochmoidart; Alexander MacDonald Esq., of Rhue; Angus MacDonald Esq., the younger, of Glenaladale; and the Rev. Angus McLaine, minister.

Sir James Riddell agreed to give a site for a new church in a less exposed position. Plans were drawn up and estimates obtained.

The Presbytery of Mull requested two churches but Sir James made the following offer:

'That if his plan is adopted, he would subscribe the sum of £200 towards it and he expected the rest of the committee to subscribe according to their means, but shall not exceed £800. If two churches were demanded this offer shall not stand.'

The 'new' church is now almost 160 years old. The design is essentially that proposed by William Burn, the Edinburgh architect, in 1827, though certain details of the tower are not precisely as envisaged by Burn. Originally too the church had three entrances though one of them, that in the west wall, was blocked off some years ago.

The side galleries and the Laird's Gallery opposite the raised pulpit give the plan a T-form, the pulpit arranged at a height that put the preacher and the laird on the same level and the congregation below. The custom of having a specific place in the church for each township, for communions and weddings particularly, continued until about fifty years ago. The Laird's Gallery was furnished with easy chairs and a couch and was carpeted.

Though reputed to have come from Napoleon's drawing room on St Helena the couch and chairs were probably of much later date and donated by another laird.

At the same time it was decided that the manse would have to be replaced to make a more comfortable and commodious residence for the minister, as the old manse was considered to be beyond repair; so a new building was added to the front of the old one.

In 1839 Mr McLaine's health deteriorated and he wanted to retire. The Presbytery was unwilling to lose his services and granted him 18 months leave of absence in order to make a visit to Australia. Sir James Riddell was not agreeable to this and disapproved of the Presbytery's action and they were cited to appear with Mr McLaine before the next Assembly. Nine members of the Presbytery attended and after a speech by the Moderator, John MacLeod, (in favour of Mr McLaine, who was not present), it was found that there was no ground for complaint.

Mr McLaine retired, however, in 1841 and returned home to live at Fascadale, Ardrishaig, until his death in December 1877. He was unmarried.

Archibald Clerk was presented in July 1837. His presentation is reported to have been by Queen Victoria but it is unclear whether this was an intervention by Her Majesty personally or by a Crown Official acting on her behalf. Mr Clerk was ordained at Acharacle in 1838 before going to Duirinish in Skye in 1840. He was in Kilchoan from 1841 to 1844 and presented the Second Statistical account for Ardnamurchan and Sunart which had been drawn up earlier by Mr McLaine.

David Stewart was a man of original character, a scholar and a theologian. He was admitted to the parish in 1844 and erected, at his own expense, a church and schoolhouse at Kilmory, about 5 miles from Kilchoan. After being out of use since the 1970s the church was closed in 1989 and sold into private ownership.

A pew from Kilmory was placed in Kilchoan Church where an inscribed plaque commemorates the closure.

A closing service was held in 1989 at the tiny church. One of the congregation was a Norwegian widower, Mr Bob Fjortoft, who married his late wife Joan there just after the last world war, the couple being the last to be married in that church.

David Stewart was found dead in bed on 8 May 1860 and is buried beside the front door of the present church in Kilchoan.

Donald MacFadyen succeeded Mr Stewart on transfer to Kilchoan from Acharacle in 1860 and was himself suceeded through the transfer of Lachlan MacLean from Arisaig in 1870. After he left in 1878, Robert Munro was admitted to the church in 1879 and stayed until 1890 when he went to Dervaig on Mull.

John Smith, who was born in 1839, was admitted to the parish in 1890. His father was a farmer and Mr Smith farmed the Glebe as well as attending to his church duties. He kept cows for milking, and some sheep as well as poultry. He must have been a gentleman of some means since he employed in the household two housemaids and a butler. He had six children, all but the youngest being sent to Edinburgh to be educated.

Mrs Smith played the organ in the church and both the church and the manse were kept in very good repair, and money was spent on the fabric of both. Mr Smith did not have very much Gaelic but was quite determined to hold some of his services in that language so he learned it but never became very fluent.

After the retirement of John Smith in 1926, Neil MacDonald, a Hebridean from North Uist, came to the parish from Tiree. He married locally and had two sons and was the writer of the Third Statistical Account for Ardnamurchan.

It is not easy to do justice to the contribution Mr MacDonald made to the life and style of the community. During his many years as minister, and afterwards during his retirement in Kilchoan, he became greatly esteemed and much loved. He represented Ardnamurchan on Argyll County Council and was the first Assessor for Ardnamurchan appointed by the Crofters' Commission when that office was created.

The generosity and hospitality of Mr MacDonald and his wife Mary were renowned. For example, it was the practice for local cars to collect worshippers from the more distant parts of the parish to take them to church. On communion Sundays it became routine for the cars to take those members of the congregation from church to the manse for lunch; hospitality continued to be shown until it was time for the return journey to church for evening service.

Mr MacDonald retired in 1962 but continued to live in Kilchoan until his death in 1978. He is buried in the old graveyard.

The charge became vacant at Mr MacDonald's retirement and remained so for some time. Mr Alec Ingram, a retired minister living in Acharacle, agreed to come to Kilchoan and take the church services.

At that time it was decided that the manse was again in a very bad state of repair and a new manse in the form of a modern bungalow was erected on the Glebe. The old building and the remainder of the Glebe land were sold.

The first occupant of the new manse was Mr Harold Ferrie who in 1967 was inducted to the parish and remained there until he retired in 1975.

With the decline in population the congregation at the church also declined and, as it was difficult to find a minister to take Mr Ferrie's place, in 1977 the charge was linked with that of Acharacle under the ministration of Mr Andrew MacKenzie.

Thus the church had gone full circle, both Kilchoan and Acharacle again coming under the same minister. Mr MacKenzie retired in 1979 and in 1980 Mr Victor Crawford was appointed to the linked charge.

Mr Crawford initiated the Parish Newsletter. He was also instrumental in the setting-up of the Restoration Fund and of a committee which organised various commemorative events in 1981 to celebrate the 150th anniversary of the building of the church. Notable among those events was the publication of the first edition of *Ardnamurchan – Annals of the Parish*.

In January 1987 Mr Crawford was called to the parish of Calton Parkhead in Glasgow and was succeeded by Mr Tom Moffat who was inducted in that year.

The Roman Catholic Church

Despite its importance in Scottish and local history the Roman Catholic Church has little direct involvement today with the Ardnamurchan district and no church or associated building exists within the parish..

The few Roman Catholic inhabitants travel beyond the boundary to their church at Mingarry, north of the Shiel river.

The Free Church

There are no early records for the Free Church in Ardnamurchan though a clear oral tradition tells of regular services from the date of the Disruption. In summer the people met in a gravel pit and during winter in a barn at Ormsaigmore. Meetings were conducted by local leaders of the movement, by Gaelic teachers and Catechists who worked in the district, or by itinerant preachers and ministers.

There was no organised congregation until in 1864 regular preaching and 'occasional ministerial service' was ensured by the Presbytery of Lorn and Mull. In 1868 the work was granted the status of a preaching station with its own elders and Kirk Session, and regular Communion services. Written records with Rolls of Communicants and Adherents were instituted though sadly these disappeared in the events of 1900.

The congregation was raised to the status of a Sanctioned Charge by the General Assembly of 1873. Being without state funding the Free Church was responsible for supporting its own ministers and the schedule submitted by the Presbytery to the General Assembly in that year noted that there was a Sustentation Fund with five collectors and 140 contributors.

There was no Free Church School and the nearest Free Church was that at Strontian, the famous 'floating church'.

Thirty-three years after the Disruption a church and manse were built at Kilchoan on land provided by local crofters from the Common Grazings.

The foundation-stone was laid in 1876 and the church, described in contemporary reports as a 'plain but elegant edifice' was built by Messrs MacDougall and MacColl of Oban.

The church already had a minister, Nicol Campbell, who had been inducted in 1874. He ministered there until translated to Uig, Lewis, in 1889. He was succeeded by James MacNiven, who served the congregation until in 1900 he went, with the majority of Free Church ministers, into the uniting body which became the United Free Church.

The congregation though remained in the Free Church and was served by resident Lay Preachers throughout the long vacancy which followed.

The list of ordained ministers in this century is an interesting one. It includes Kenneth Taylor, from England – the first non-Gaelic-speaking minister, and Hugh MacCallum who was born and brought up in Ormsaigmore. The present minister, Revd Graeme Craig, was ordained and inducted to the charge in October 1989.

Happily, relationships between the two churches in the Ardnamurchan district, their respective ministers and the people of the congregations have always been congenial and continue so to the present day.

3

PEOPLE, PLACES AND FACTS

A long peninsula of solid rock,
upholstered every year in threadbare green.
Stones everywhere, ambiguous and burgeoning.
In Sanna ramparts of them march around our crofts
but whether to keep cattle out or other stones
no man can say.
And at Kilchoan there were three houses
cropped from one field.
That was when I was a boy.
The masons left the pebbles
and there's a castle now, waiting to be harvested.
God was short of earth when He made Ardamurchan.

ALASDAIR MACLEAN

The long history of Ardnamurchan is enriched by many tales, some of people who have inhabited the peninsula over the centuries, others of places, many renowned beyond its bounds. Space limitations allow the presentation of only a part of the story.

Crofting and the Highland Clearances.

The old ruined crofts on the hillside remind me,
The memory binds me, I weep for their pain,
But the sons of the Clans the world o'er know the story
And dream of the road to Kilchoan again.

HELEN ANDREW

Apart from minor changes the crofting system as we know it now has existed for a little over a hundred years. Its earlier origins lie in the old Highland clan system which allowed the natives to occupy small parcels of land in return for serving the clan chief.

Due to economic conditions that system was largely discontinued after the Jacobite Rising of 1745 at which time it was deemed necessary to introduce lowland sheep farmers who paid economic rents, the native population being evicted to provide pasture for sheep farming.

There followed, for those evicted, long periods of hardship and forced emigration about which many authors have written at length.

In 1883 the government appointed the Napier Commission to study the Highland problem. After a lengthy survey the Commission recommended that crofters should have security of tenure. This was introduced when the Crofters Holdings (Scotland) Act of 1886 gave perpetual tenancy subject to the prompt payment of rent, an aspect of croft legislation which has continued to the present time. The Act also gave the right to a fair negotiated rent and provided for compensation to the crofter for improvements carried out during his tenancy.

The Crofters Commission was formed in 1955. The Commission compiled a register of crofts and co-operates with land-owners in croft assignations and re-lettings and various items of crofting legislation. Since the regularisation, legal matters have been dealt with by the Scottish Land Court which evolved from the Napier Commission in 1886.

The recently formed Crofters Union has been successful in highlighting the many problems confronting crofters and the need for government investment in the crofting areas.

The following note by Alex MacKenzie was written in 1914. As the above paragraphs make clear, such evictions as the writer describes could not take place today.

"Uaine gu'm mullach – green to their tops." So Dr Norman MacLeod described the bens of Ardnamurchan in his inimitable sketch, the *Emigrant Ship*, and so they appear even to this day. Their beautiful slopes show scarcely a vestige of heather but an abundance of rich, sweet grass of a quality suitable for pasturage.

"As the steamboat passenger sails northward through the Sound of Mull he sees straight ahead, and stretching at right angles across his course, a long range of low hills culminating in a finely-shaped mass which seems to rise abruptly from the edge of the sea. The hills are those of Ardnamurchan, and the dominating pile is Ben Hiant, 1729 feet in height, and 'green to its top'. Around the base of the mountain and for miles in every direction the land is fair, fertile, and well adapted either for arable or grazing purposes. It comprises the farm of Mingary, and today [1914] is wholly under deer.

"Down to the second decade of last century it supported about twenty-six families, which were distributed over the component townships of Coiremhuilinn, Skinid, Buarblaig and Tornamona. At one sweep, the whole place was cleared, and the grounds added to

[27]

the adjacent sheep farm at Mingary.

"The evictions were carried out in 1828, the process being attended with many acts of heartless cruelty on the part of the Laird's representatives. In one case a half-witted woman who flatly refused to flit, was locked up in her cottage, the door being barricaded on the outside by mason-work. She was visited every morning to see if she had arrived at a tractable frame of mind, but for days she held out. It was not until her slender store of food was exhausted that she ceased to argue with the inevitable and decided to capitulate. It is to cases of this character that Dr John MacLachlan, the Sweet Singer of Rahoy, referred in the lines:

> 'An dall, an seann duine san oinid
> Toirt am mallachd air do bhuaireas'

> (The blind, the aged and the imbecile
> Calling curses on thy greed.)

"The proprietor at whose instance these 'removals' were carried out was Sir James Milles Riddell, Bart. Of the dislodged families a few were given small patches of waste land, some were given holdings in various townships on the estate – the crofts of which were subdivided for their accommodation – and some were forced to seek sanctuary beyond the Atlantic.

"Additional clearances were effected on the Ardnamurchan estate in 1853, when Swordle-chaol, Swordle-mhor and Swordle-chorrach, with an aggregate area of about 3000 acres, were divested of their crofting population and thrown into a single sheep farm. Swordle-chaol was occupied by four tenants, Swordle-mhor by six, and Swordle-chorrach by six. Five years previous to the evictions, all the crofters came under a written obligation to the proprietor to build new dwelling houses. The walls were to be of stone and lime, 40 ft long, 17½ ft wide and 7½ ft high. The houses, two-gabled, were to have each two rooms and a kitchen alone to be floored with flags. By the end of 1851 all the tenants had faithfully implemented their promise, and the work of the building was quite completed. Tradesmen had been employed in every case and the cost averaged from £45 to £50.

"When the people were ejected two years later they received no compensation whatever for their labours and outlays. They were not even permitted to remove a door, a window or fixed cupboard.

Some of the houses are still intact in this year of grace, 1914, one being occupied by a shepherd on Swordle farm, and another used as a byre. They compare favourably as regards size, design and workmanship with the best and most modern crofter houses in the Ardnamurchan district.

"The Swordle tenants were among the best-to-do on the estate, and not one of them owed the proprietor a shilling in the way of arrears of rent. When cast adrift, the majority of them were assigned 'holdings' of one acre or so in the rough lands of Sanna and Portuairk, where they had to start to reclaim peat bogs and to build for themselves house and steadings. Sir James Milles Riddell was the proprietor responsible for clearing the Swordles as well as the Ben Hiant townships.

"About 16 years ago [about 1898] Ben Hiant, or Mingary, as well as the Swordles, Laga, Tarbert and other farms were swept clean of sheep and converted into a deer forest, the preserve having a total area of 22,000 acres.

"The wooly ruminants met with retribution, direful and complete, and the native people viewed the change with mild amusement. Sheep had been the means of ruining their forefathers, whereas deer had never done them or their kinsfolk the smallest injury."

Inevitably the mists of time conceal the truth of some stories or sometimes, blown aside by the breeze of new evidence, allow that truth to appear. A story was told that in the mid-19th century, the then proprietor Mr Dalgleish refused to renew the lease of a tenant farmer in Ormsaigmore because of his taking up the cause of the farmers.

The tacksman, Mr McColl, found the eviction difficult and had to send to Oban for soldiers and a court officer to carry it out. As the farmer's bedridden wife was being carried from the house she cursed the tacksman, saying that when he died no grass would grow on his grave, only dockens and nettles. McColl's grave stands by the front of the old church and nothing grows on it.

In fact, Mr McColl could not have been involved, having died in 1847, years before the incident which is known to have a much more recent dating. The eviction resulted, not from what we might today call militant activism, but from the more mundane fault of failing to pay the rent.

While it is true that grass does not grow on the grave that is because of the flat stone, surrounded by iron railings, which covers it.

Vikings and others before and since.

Another old tale has faded under the glare of recent examination. It tells of Somerled and the men of Morvern killing a number of Norwegian chiefs including Borrodill, reputed to have been seven feet tall. Local legend places his grave close to the Allt Innis nam Feorag (the stream of the valley of the squirrels) and it is suggested that he gave his name to Glen Borrodale.

While the latter may well be true, the so-called grave is now believed to be the remains of an old corn-mill dating only from some time in the last century.

Another legend explains the absence of swans from Loch Sunart. In ancient days a young Celtic chieftain fell in love with a local girl of much more humble birth. The match was fiercely opposed by the lad's mother who, using magical powers, turned the girl into a swan. The young man found and killed the swan during a hunting trip and was horrified to find the beautiful bird taking in death the human form of his love. He killed himself with his own sword so that the two could lie together beneath the waters of Sunart. Swans today are understandably reluctant to be found in the Sunart area.

The name MacIain is an important one in the Ardnamurchan story and not all the legends concern the warlike activity of the clansmen. One McIain built an unenviable reputation as a cattle-thief, earning the enmity of his main victim, MacLean of Duart.

But MacIain one day surprised three witches sticking pins into an effigy of MacLean. Taking the effigy quickly to the MacLean home, where he found the chief dying, he removed each pin. At the extraction of the final pin MacLean rose, restored to health, and enmity was readily converted to friendship.

Anecdotal extracts from press reports are often a valuable source of information on contemporary attitudes and problems. The following, taken from the Oban Times in 1904, gives an insight into divisions which existed in society at that time:

'At a meeting of the Ardnamurchan School Board held on Friday, Mr TJA Armstrong, factor for Mr CD Rudd, presiding, a motion to the effect that all applications for the use of schoolhouses for social meetings should in future be refused, was for the second time submitted by the Rev John Smith and seconded by the Rev James MacNiven.

Mr John Campbell moved the previous question and was proceeding to address the meeting when –

MR CAMPBELL – My amendment is quite competent, as I shall endeavour to prove if you give me an opportunity to express my views.

Mr MacNiven reiterated that the amendment could not be discussed.

MR CAMPBELL – I ask you, Mr Chairman, whether my amendment is or is not competent.

THE CHAIRMAN – I am afraid, Mr MacNiven, you shall have to keep quiet. The amendment is perfectly in order.

Mr Campbell observed that it entirely depended on the vote of the chairman who was not present at the last meeting, when this matter was first discussed whether the retrograde action of the clerical faddists was to bear fruit or not. The local feeling, as they were all aware, was keenly antagonistic to the schoolhouses being closed against social and political meetings, and if the estate management were going to ignore that feeling the consequences might be serious and far-reaching.

THE CHAIRMAN – No personalities, please.

MR CAMPBELL – As for the ministers –

MR MACMILLAN (interrupting) – The ministers can draw their stipends in spite of everybody; nevertheless, we will make them scratch their heads yet. (Laughter).

After a heated discussion, lasting over two hours, the vote was taken and the motion carried by three votes to two.

Mr Campbell said he regretted that the chairman had deemed it expedient to assume an attitude distinctly hostile to the crofter sentiment. Within a week, he ventured to predict, the heather would be on fire in Ardnamurchan, just as it had blazed in the '80s.

A MEMBER – Surely you do not mean to adopt a policy of retaliation

MR CAMPBELL – It is certainly a pity to disturb the harmony which has subsisted for years between laird and crofter on the estate, but I fear much that after the decision at which this Board has just arrived, a crofter upheaval can scarcely be avoided

The meeting terminated amid cries of "Withdraw" and "Shame"'.

Though thus deprived of the use of their school for social gatherings the local people were determined to have somewhere to meet on such occasions and a fund-raising programme opened.

Events including such functions as barn dances were held not only in local steadings and the shop garage but in the inn. The inn served too as a venue for wedding receptions. Door to door collections added to the funds and eventually, thanks to those sustained local efforts and to what was described at the time as a 'handsome donation' from Sir Kenneth Clark, the Kilchoan Hall opened in November 1930.

Mingary Pier and its Origins

Earlier Oban Times reports give details of how Mingary pier was erected and indicate the difficulties which followed.

A report in 1890 noted that 'the West Highland Commission has been asked to visit the district to discuss the building of a pier and the funding thereof.'

A year and a half later slow progress had been made as the Oban Times reported that 'at a meeting regarding the building of a pier at Mingary, Mr Ferguson, tenant of Mingary, granted permission without compensation for access to the proposed site of the pier. It was unanimously decided to have the pier at Port na Mairbh, Mingary.'

But the problems remained. In June 1892 the paper noted that 'the landing place proposed for Mingary pier has not been accepted for the present, the total cost being above the £2,000 limit'.

However, in mid-1893 the Secretary of State for Scotland intervened to suggest a grant of £1,800 towards the cost if local sources would guarantee the remaining £200. That sum was raised easily, the estate proprietor, Mr Dalgleish, donating most of it.

Five years later the pier was completed (at a mere 10% above the original estimate) though the saga did not end there. A 1901 Oban Times reports on yet another meeting:

'This pier, which was completed early in 1898 at a cost of £2200 to serve as a place of call for the mail and cargo steamers calling at Ardnamurchan has as yet been of no benefit to the district, as Mr MacBrayne demurs to using it, but continues to call with his steamers at Kilchoan Bay as formerly. With a view to remedy this state of matters, a largely attended meeting was held at Kilchoan School on Wednesday last.

'Rev Mr Smith, parish minister, presided, and stated that the Mingary Pier was built about three years ago at a cost of £2000. Of this sum the Government had provided £1696, while the balance had been subscribed locally. In consequence, however, of some sunken rocks lying in the channel leading to the pier, its navigation by vessels of large draught was attended with some degree of danger, but in the case of steamers of light draught this danger entirely vanished.

'Mr MacBrayne had declined to allow any of his steamers to call at this pier, and goods, mails and passengers continued to be landed by means of the old fashioned ferry boat, ferry dues being imposed at the rate of threepence per head and on goods at a similar rate per article.

'Mr CD Rudd of Ardnamurchan had generously offered to disburse pound for pound with the Government in order to extend and improve the pier. (Applause). This offer had been unfortunately disregarded by the Secretary for Scotland. These circumstances constituted a serious grievance, and no effort should be spared to remove it. (Applause).

'Mr Colthart, Achateny, the largest farmer in the parish said they had only themselves to blame for their present position. As a result of a strong agitation they had succeeded in getting the pier built, and towards its construction the government gave a grant of £1696, the County Council £310, and the local contribution amounted to £216.

'For all that money there was as yet no return; no steamer touched at the pier, but continued landing and embarking goods at Kilchoan Bay by the old ferry boat, the owner of which levied a charge, 3d on every passenger and parcel conveyed in his boat. This detestable exaction was becoming unbearable as it was simply "payin' for a drookin" as both their person and their goods were often much injured by this mode of landing.

'He thought that they should respectfully approach Mr MacBrayne and ask him to call at the pier with his steamers and if he should refuse them they could approach other companies who might be expected to call. The goods landed at Kilchoan averaged close upon 4 tons weekly, and that along with the large passenger traffic which would enormously increase if the pier was used, was worth catering for. He trusted this large meeting would bear some fruit.

'Mr Malcolm MacMillan, Merchant, followed and advised the forming of a committee who would rent the pier from the County

Council.

'The present tenant was the owner of the ferry-boat and it was to his advantage to have the pier closed. There was no use in saying the pier was dangerous and risky to approach for they had all seen the various steamers on the route occasionally calling for cattle and sheep, and quite recently the Staffa took the pier on as stormy a day as was seldom experienced. He hoped that they would never rest till the pier was made a regular place of call.

'Messrs James Cameron, Glendryden; David MacPhee, Achosnich; Dugald MacDiarmid, Ormsaig; and several others followed in the same strain and eventually a strong and influential committee was formed with the Rev Mr Smith as convener to take all the necessary steps to get the steamers to call at the pier.

'The committee met immediately after the general meeting and resolved to ask Mr MacBrayne to cause his steamers to call at the pier. In the event of an unsatisfactory reply the committee intend to approach another Glasgow shipping company.

'A proposal to rent the pier from the County Council and to apply for a provisional order subjecting to pier dues all goods landed within a certain radius on either side of the pier was left over till the next meeting.'

The meeting was less than fair to MacBraynes in suggesting that the infamous rocks were no barrier to vessels calling for cattle and sheep. MacBraynes' case was that the rock was a hazard except at high tide, which would clearly militate against a scheduled run while allowing unscheduled trips timed to coincide with the tides. On the other hand there is evidence that the company called on the convenient excuse of the rocks when a proposed unscheduled run was likely to lead to a freight load of unprofitable quantity.

Commenting on the facilities for landing by sea at Kilchoan, Miss M. E. M. Donaldson, in *Further Wanderings in the Western Isles* makes scathingly clear that the situation continued up to the time of her writing in 1926. Indeed, it was only after the second world war that the use of vessels of a different design made a reasonable service possible.

Even today there is considerable unhappiness among West Ardnamurchan people because the Kilchoan-Tobermory ferry operates only during the summer months. This deprives them of the facilties for shopping and other services offered by a short crossing to Mull rather than the hundred-mile alternative to Fort William.

Alasdair Mac Mhaighstir Alasdair

In 1982, members of the 1745 Association gathered at Dalilea House and a plaque, reading as follows, was fixed to the wall.

"At Dalilea House in the year 1700 was born Alexander MacDonald, known as Alasdair Mac Mhaighstir Alasdair, son of Rev. Alexander MacDonald, minister of Island Finnan, the greatest of all Gaelic poets. Erected by members of the 1745 Association to commemorate the repeal in 1782 of the Disclothing Act of 1747. Am Breacan Uallach."

Alasdair MacDonald was certainly one of the most important of the 18th century Gaelic poets. His early education came from his father, Rev. Alexander MacDonald, minister of Eilean Fhianain and Ardnamurchan, who gave him a thorough grounding in English and Gaelic and in the classics. He learned to write in the Gaelic script and was steeped in the history of the Gaelic bards.

He began to compose poetry while very young. Much of his early work was descriptive of the countryside in which he had grown up, mainly round Dalilea, Loch Shiel and Castle Tioram. He wrote too of the area in Uist where he had spent summer holidays with his uncle and cousins. One of those cousins was Flora MacDonald, famous for her part in helping Prince Charles Edward to escape after the 1745 Rising.

Early records show that in 1729 Alasdair was appointed by the Society for the Propagation of Christian Knowledge as a teacher and catechist (cf. Gaelic ceister, questioner) at Eilean Fhianain. He went later to Ardnamurchan where he was given a house and some land in the township of Coiremhuillin, about half a mile from Mingary Castle.

While he was catechist he worked on Saturdays, Sundays and Mondays, his duties involving the teaching of the Shorter Catechism to both young and old and the preparation of parents for the Sacrement of Baptism.

In 1730 Alasdair wrote to the estate proprietor, Sir Alexander Murray of Stanhope, asking if he could have a school at Kilmory where there were 'forty children fit for teaching'. After much negotiation involving Sir Alexander and the Presbytery of Mull and Lorn, Alasdair opened his school in Kilmory with a salary of £18 per annum. The salary was paid by the SPCK and in order to qualify for it Alasdair was required to become a Protestant.

While living in Coiremhuillin Alasdair prepared the first Gaelic-English dictionary, described as a 'work of great merit and usefulness in schools'.

Its main purpose was to aid the teaching of English to the Gaelic-speaking adults and children in the belief that the ability to speak English would open up new opportunities for employment in varied spheres.

His collected poems were published in 1751. One of his earliest, Allt-An T-Siucair (The Sugar Brook), was dedicated 'to a special township in Ardnamurchan called Coiremhuillin and to a little stream that runs through that township, called 'Allt an-t-Siucair'.

The view is widely held that as a descriptive poem it is perhaps unequalled in any language. The first stanza gives an indication of the theme:

> A dol thar Allt-an-t-siucair
> Air maduinn chubhraidh Cheit
> 'S paideirean geal dluth-chnap
> De'n driuchd ghorm air an fheur;
> Bha Richard 's Robin Bru-Dhearg
> Ri seinn 's fear dhiu 'na bheus
> 'S goichmoit air cuthaig chul-ghuirm
> 'S gug-gug aic' air a gheig.

> (Going across the sugar brook
> One morning sweet in May
> The dew so bright like clustered beads
> Upon the green grass lay;
> Richard and Robin Redbreast
> A duet sang in tune
> And the proud cuckoo of blue-grey hue
> On the branch sang sweet all day.)

In 1744 there was much talk of a Jacobite Rising and one report states that Alasdair sent two poems to Prince Charles Edward encouraging him to come to Scotland. For most of the summer of 1744 Alasdair was absent from home and his son Ronald acted as his substitute at the school while his father became more and more active, travelling about the country as a political agent. In May 1745 he left his school for the last time, his teaching days over.

His dream was for Gaelic independence and it is said that when the Prince arrived at Loch nam Uamh one of the first persons to meet him was Alasdair Mac Mhaighster Alasdair.

They made their way to Kinlochmoidart House and were led to the jetty at Dalilea from which they sailed up Loch Shiel to Glenaladale and on 19 August 1745 raised the Standard at Glenfinnan.

Alasdair was the first to be commissioned in the Prince's army and became official bard to the Prince. Afterwards, as a reward for his services, Clanranald appointed him Baillie in the Isle of Canna in 1749 and he and his family lived there until 1751 while he continued to write poetry.

Later he settled in Sandaig where he wrote his epic poem, *Birlin Chlann Raghnaill* (Clanranald's Galley), its 556 lines making it the longest poem in the Gaelic language.

Alasdair died in 1770. It had been intended to carry his body to Eilean Fhianain but a severe gale prevented that and he was buried in the cemetery of Kilmorie near the Roman Catholic church of Arisaig.

Charles Dunnel Rudd of Glenborrodale Castle.

One of the leading figures in the modern history of the peninsula also had a vital though largely unacknowledged role in British colonial history. A very strong case can be made for suggesting that Charles Rudd's part in the creation of Rhodesia, indeed in the creation of Rhode's own reputation, was at least as great as that of Rhodes himself.

Rhodes spent eight years studying at Oxford and it was Rudd who made it possible for him to go there and to stay. Rudd accepted responsibility for keeping going, in Kimberly, Rhodes's business interests for the 'Oxford' years, as well as continuing on his return to give him sound business advice.

It was Rudd who, at considerable personal risk, negotiated the Manatee mining concession which was a cornerstone of the whole Rhodesian story. Yet Rudd's name is absent from reference works which devote considerable space to Rhodes.

FR 'Matabele' Thompson, himself well-known for his involvement in Rhodesian affairs, was a friend of Rhodes and said of Rudd: 'Rhodes placed the greatest reliance on his friend Rudd. Rudd indeed was a great man. He was never known to be connected with a crooked deal. He was able, honest, good-tempered and clean-living, a man of whom his descendants may well be proud.'

That was the man who built Glenborrodale Castle. He was married twice. His first wife died before the Castle was finished. Rudd himself died, aged 72, in 1916 and his second wife in 1951. They are buried at Acharacle.

Rudd did much for the tenants on his land and made great improvements to the roads. With the object of improving the domestic amenities of his tenants, he proposed what may be regarded as an admirable housing scheme. A loan of £80 free of interest and to be repaid over a period of 14 years was offered to each crofter for re-building or repairing his house, though only four took advantage of the offer.

Refusal to participate in it was due, it is believed, to the animus against all landlords, whom the crofters in the light of bitter experience would not trust.

Time however softened the bitterness and housing improvements initiated by Lord Trent at a later date were welcomed.

Sanna

Before there was a churchyard on soft ground
at Kilchoan, or carts to carry bodies to it,
there were folks at Sanna. When they died
their followers could find no earth with depth
for even a shallow grave. They had a choice
between bog and beach and who'd want the bog,
to lie suspended through the centuries
with every scar still ready for the probe
and every wrinkle signalling. It's politic
to shed flesh while the shedding's good
and hope for a better fit next time.
They chose the beach and there they are today
under the short turf. No stone within a mile of them,
only the weight of time and the wind's slow curiosity.
I could wish my own bones, when I hand them back,
so soft a bed, so sweet and cool a resurrection.

ALASDAIR MACLEAN

Ruined walls, cairns and mounds, lazy beds and other evidence of enclosures and field systems indicate the presence of early settlements at Sanna. In August 1926 'cremation burials' were discovered in the sand dunes. The burned bones were surrounded by small stones but without evidence of date. Shards of beakerware, a barbed and tanged flint arrowhead, two flint knives or scrapers and two axeheads were also found and are now in the University Museum of Archaeology and Ethnology, Cambridge.

On the rocky headland, Rubha an Duin Bhain (the point of the white fort), the remains of what may have been a fortress and the ruins of a stone wall built across the base of the promontory are still visible. Immediately to the north of the wall are two grassy shelves on which dwellings may have stood.

In 1815 the Gaelic School Society opened a Gaelic school on the Bealach Ruadh, a central spot chosen because from it radiated tracks to the many settlements, including one to Plocaig and Sanna.

The census of 1841, however, reveals that Sanna did not at first send pupils. It had not become established as a settlement, being used by the estate and looked after by one man.

The next census in 1891 discloses a considerable shift in population. Sanna now had 22 homes, with 85 people, chiefly those 'cleared' from Ben Hiant.

The district was peopled by folk who had lived through a troubled half century. They had seen the clearances, the failure of the potato crop in 1847, and emigration of family and friends. Many had found themselves homeless, penniless, lacking proper food and clothing, suffering illnesses for which there were neither remedies nor medical care.

Yet they surmounted most of their difficulties, built homes and boats for themselves and, organising a system of cultivation for their crofts, gradually became almost self-sufficient.

Sanna was divided into two, the Bail' Iosal and the Bail' Ard (the Lower Farm and the Higher Farm). The agricultural land was shared on the runrig system, with separate holdings of small strips of arable land lying between those of different joint tenants to ensure a fair distribution of good and indifferent land. Sanna appears to have been on the system of fixed runrig, strips being permanently associated with a single holding.

Much of the work was done by the women since many of the men were sea-faring or in other ways forced to seek a wage away from home. Each family had one cow though because of the lush grazing one cow at Sanna could be usefully productive, yielding milk, butter and crowdies. The calves were reared to a certain age then sent to market.

The women gathered carrageen and dulse from the shore and among the rocks found whelks, limpets, mussels, oysters and crabs. From these they were able to make substantial meals with the addition of milk, butter and sometimes oatmeal.

Life was a routine of feeding and clothing families, and of cutting peats to give winter fuel, bracken to bed cattle, and marram grass for thatching.

There must have been time for relaxation because tales of pastimes survive. Sanna became a gathering place for the youth of the area. Teams of boys from Kilchoan played shinty against teams from the Roinn (The Point District) gathering each weekend on Dail Shana for this, or for contests of strength including clach neart (putting the stone), maide leisg (a form of wrestling), running, jumping, and the caber. There were competitions too in bardachd, (poetry making), story-telling and dancing.

Nevertheless they were people who in the latter half of the 19th century were deprived both physically and spiritually. Because the Point District – Sanna, Achnaha and Achosnich – had no proper road to Kilchoan nor any means of transport few were able to attend the churches at Kilchoan.

After a successful mission carried out by preachers from the Faith Mission who lived in the community for some weeks, held gospel meetings, and visited families in their homes, a religous revival led to the building of the Sanna Mission Hall which exists still.

Built about 1890, it was a non-denominational place of worship used by the ministers of the Free Church and the Church of Scotland in alternate weeks. Services were usually in Gaelic with a precentor giving out the line of the psalm.

The Hall was regularly used by Church of Scotland ministers until the gradual depopulation of the area, and the linking of the Acharacle and Ardnamurchan parishes, caused abandonment of services. Yet even today visiting ministers sometimes hold services for the increased summer population.

In 1925 Miss M.E.M. Donaldson, the writer and photographer, settled here after visiting the area many times and making many friends. She obtained written consent from each of the Sanna crofters to buy land; without that consent the Scottish Land Court would not have allowed her the site.

Some materials for her house were conveyed to a nearby beach by puffers though local stone was used for the building and the roof was thatched with heather. Unskilled assistance for the builders was given by local crofters. The house was completed in 1927 and was called Sanna Bheag (Little Sanna).

Miss Donaldson took a keen interest in local affairs, helping to improve amenities while preserving the peace and charm of the area. In 1929 she launched a public protest about the condition of the 20-mile stretch of road between Kilchoan and Salen. She also helped the crofters in their efforts to have a road between Achnaha and Sanna constructed by the government.

Her best-known books on the Highlands and their history are *Wanderings in the Western Highlands and Islands* and *Further Wanderings Mainly in Argyll*. Her photographs are an invaluable record of life in the area during her sojourn here.

Miss Donaldson left Sanna at about the start of the second world war. During the war years Sanna Bheag was occupied by tenants but in 1947 the roof caught fire and the whole building except the exterior walls was destroyed.

In 1948 there were still 14 occupied houses in Sanna. 18 pensioners from there were among 35 who collected their weekly pensions from the Post Office at Achosnich. As the years passed and the old population died and the young people sought work elsewhere, the croft houses changed hands.

Many have been bought as holiday homes and have been improved in appearance and comfort and saved from becoming derelict. There are today 14 holiday homes, and one house which is occupied throughout the year.

Another writer who lived at Sanna for some years was Alasdair MacLean, several of whose poems are reproduced in these pages. He has been writing poetry almost since boyhood, mainly on rural subjects, on changing scenes, and on reminiscences of Ardnamurchan. He has published three volumes of verse: *From the Wilderness*, *Waking the Dead* and *Poetry Introduction Two*. *From the Wilderness* won two major literary awards. His first non-fiction book, *Night Falls on Ardnamurchan*, was published in 1984 and follows his father's journal with Alasdair's own commentary.

Achosnich

Achosnich – the field of the sighing winds – is known to have been inhabited as early as 2000 BC. There are signs of an early settlement at Cnoc Nitheadrechd, a wooded knoll in the valley between Achosnich and Sonachan.

The late Alex Stewart, while excavating a road to the Achosnich schoolhouse in 1952, found a stone axe-head which was dated by the Museum of Antiquities in Edinburgh as 2000 BC. A very early millstone found below Sonachan is in the safe keeping of Mr and Mrs MacPhail at the Sonachan hotel.

The road between Achosnich and Portuairk was built in 1950-51 by Irish workers billeted in the Achosnich school. The school had been closed in 1945 and the pupils transferred to Kilchoan. Prior to the construction of the road the women of Portuairk carried their provisions in sacks on their backs from Achosnich, bulk supplies of flour, salt and tea being purchased yearly from a travelling salesman.

Cnoc Catriona and Tobar (well) Catriona are named after a young woman killed by a stag while wood-gathering below Sonachan in about 1890. At the time, stags were being fed to encourage growth of the antlers; the more points on the antlers the more prized they were as trophies. The stag may have attacked Catriona in the belief that she was carrying food.

The land on which the township of Portuairk stands was gifted by the crofters of Achosnich to families who had been evicted from more fertile lands. An Achosnich crofter, Malcolm MacMillan, was a prominent figure in the Scottish Land League, the organisation which eventually brought about the passing of the Act of 1886 under which crofters' rights were recognised.

Sonachan, near Achosnich, was originally called An Aodann, the face. The MacPhee family who were crofters at An Aodain became tenants of Horsley Hall, Strontian, which today is the Sunart Hotel.

The desire to preserve the Gaelic tongue by encouraging its teaching in schools is not a modern one. Records show that in 1891 Mr John Campbell, secretary of the Ardnamurchan Land League, was congratulated on his successful efforts to have the language taught in Ardnamurchan schools.

An 1891 report by one of Her Majesty's Inspectors concerning Achosnich school throws interesting light on the rural schooling of the time.

'An epidemic interrupted the work of the school for a consider-able time but not withstanding, the general efficiency of the school is very gratifying. The senior pupils are taught by the Schoolmaster and 14 older pupils are proficient in Latin and Navigation. The number of passes in written Gaelic is 7. The junior division is taught by the Schoolmaster's wife and does excellent work, the girls being taught cookery and needlework of a high standard.

'The Gaelic Society of London have forwarded to Mr John Campbell a number of valuable Gaelic books, MacAlpine's Gaelic Dictionary, Mackenzie's History of Scotland, Clarsach na Coille, etc.'

Portuairk

Portuairk

The name Portuairk was originally Port-na-Gruaigean. Gruaigean is thought to be Gaelic for a species of seaweed. Apparently Portuairk had an abundance of this type of seaweed which has a long stalk and is sweet to taste, so much so that people actually chewed the stalks. Through the years, the present name has evolved through Anglicised pronunciation.

It was roughly 150 years ago that people settled in Portuairk. Some had been cleared from as far away as Morvern and Laga. The first child to be born there was James Cameron who eventually settled in Ockle, where his descendants still live. He once achieved the tremendous feat of rowing a boat from Oban to Ockle in three days.

The people of Grigadale and Achosnich gave the ground at Portuairk to the people who settled there. It was poor ground, with trees right down to the shore. Some stayed in caves or whatever other shelter they could find until they could build houses. They cleared the ground of the trees, using the large branches as sledges to pull the huge rocks for building their houses.

Manpower they had in plenty for it was not unusual for couples to have twelve, even up to 20, children. Potatoes and fish were their main food. Portuairk in the early days had such an abundance of fish that the women could put the potatoes on to boil and then catch, with the rod, sufficient fish for that meal.

A major tragedy at Portuairk was the loss in March 1891 of Donald MacColl, a 44-year old father, and his sons Hugh, aged 15, and 13-year old Lachlan. The bodies of the two boys were never found though that of their father came ashore at Bay MacNeil. He had died of hypothermia rather than drowning. The three had been bringing seaweed from the lighthouse by sailboat to Portuairk when the weather suddenly worsened. The lighthouse keeper saw they were in difficulty and ran up Beinn Beaga to give the alarm, but nothing could be done.

The sea played a big part in the lives of the people. At one time, from the ten houses came as many as eight sea captains. Such was the determination of the local men to succeed in careers at sea that if they failed an examination they would join the children at the school for a few months, until the schoolmaster was satisfied that they were proficient in the particular subject in which they had failed.

The children were lucky having a school to attend, but for many years they had no seats or desks. They sat on stones and were not allowed to attend unless they brought a peat, which had to be of a certain size, for the fire. Anyone bringing a broken peat was given the strap.

When the road from Kilchoan to Portuairk was made, every household was required to send a man to work on it. No concession was given to households without a man, such families being compelled to provide a woman to wield the shovel alongside the men.

Kilmory

The name Kilmory (Cille-Mhoire) means the cell or church of Mary; Kilmory in Ardnamurchan shares its name with many places in Western Scotland.

An old church at Kilmory is now a ruin standing in its churchyard, though the land used for burials extended far beyond the confines of the round stone wall which now encircles the graves. This wall was erected probably about the middle of the last century. It was about that time that two priests from the Roman Catholic church at Moidart came to take away the old stone baptismal font but the local inhabitants objected so strongly that the font was left within the ruins of the church. It is said that the little font is never empty of water and that even in the driest weather there is a little moisture in the bottom.

From more recent times comes a story that a man was one day scything the grass in the churchyard when a hiker came in to look at the graves. He picked up the little font, emptied out the water, and prepared to put it in his bag. Fortunately there was someone there, and he was immediately asked to put it back, as it must never be taken away from the churchyard.

To the north-west is a small meadow known as Imire, land of the dead.

When a funeral came by boat, perhaps from as far north as Arisaig, the body was conveyed from the point where it landed at the shore straight to this field, and here the procession would halt before proceeding to the graveyard a few yards distant.

The later church at Kilmory had a missionary preacher, Archibald Downie. He lived at Caim with his wife and family and cycled each day to his church and the school. He died aged 56 years and is buried at Kilmory. His place was taken by his brother, Donald, who married a lady from Uist and also lived at Caim. He was a great personality and was very popular; there are people living in the village today who remember him with great affection. He finally went to Uist.

Crois ni Mhath is the name of the ridge to the north-east of the old churchyard. Travelling across country from that direction mourners would have their first glimpse of the churchyard from the top of this ridge. They would stop there and cross themselves; hence the name, which means 'the cross that would do good'.

Beyond the churchyard walls, across the burn near the old cart track, are two graves side by side. It is hard to distinguish their outlines now, but at the beginning of the century they were clearly marked.

One of them is known to be the grave of a man named Iain. His is the classic story of one who murdered for gold, and found out too late that he had killed his own brother. It is said that he lived with his mother somewhere in Lochaber. His brother, Alistair, had left home as a youth to seek his fortune elsewhere. Many years passed, and at last Alistair came back late at night to the old home in Lochaber, having that day or the previous day called at the home of his aunt who lived some distance away.

Perhaps because of the darkness, and lapse of time, he was unrecognised, and he passed himself off as a stranger seeking a bed. That, and the fine purse of gold sovereigns which he carried, proved his undoing, as that very night he fell victim to the axe of Iain his brother.

Some days later the aunt came to visit and the awful truth came out. Crazed with remorse Iain took to the hills, a wanderer and a fugitive, coming to Kilmory where he ended his days.

As well as being a church the old building in the churchyard served as a school and was in use as early as 1827. Then another school was built on the schoolhouse croft before the present school building was erected after 1872. It, alas, ceased to function as a schoolhouse in 1961, for the present pupils are conveyed to school in Kilchoan each day by bus and car.

Another item that should be recorded is the story of how the mails were carried in the old days. It cannot be exactly determined how long ago this would be, but it was before the road between Salen and Kilchoan was built.

The post office in this district was then at Achateny. Probably it was the very first of such to be built, and ever since then the post office in the area, whatever the location, has been known as Achateny Post Office.

A woman would carry the letters to the top of the road at the Cairn where a postman, at one time a one-armed one, would walk or perhaps ride to Salen.

Kilmory

Beyond Kilmory, on the north coast in a wide bay, there is a cave which local tradition suggests was another used by St Columba on one of his visits to Ardnamurchan. The cave has two entrances gained from a ledge. Within the first entrance there is a shallow pool. Legend tells that St Columba used it to baptise some robbers he found in the cave and converted.

There are two standing stones of basalt in a hollow between a pair of rock ridges north-west of Branault near to Kilmory.

The Pulpit Classroom, Glenborrodale

Glenborrodale School is a stone building with a single classroom. It stands in the middle of the Mission of Laga, a ten-mile stretch of land along the north shore of Loch Sunart. On the east and west gables the wooden structures under the eaves are finished with crosses.

The east end of the classroom is dominated by a box-like structure,

3½ft square and 4ft high, under the window – an unusual addition serving as a pulpit for church services.

The building results from the Education Act of 1872 when schools came under democratically elected boards which required schools to be available to all children within a three to five miles walking distance. Prior to its construction a missionary worked in the Mission. He lived in a house, erected at his own expense, almost opposite the school, where the Clan Morrison Hotel stands now.

In 1962 there were no pupils and the school was closed and sold. Later, following the growth of local rural industries, there were young families again in the area and the education authority bought back the school and re-opened it in 1967. Church services too were re-commenced.

After a further short closure, the school re-opened in 1986 for three local children with a temporary teacher. A permanent teacher was appointed in the following year and by 1989 the roll had risen to nine.

Though the building was once the centre for community activity the necessarily prior claims of school-work now fill the limited space and restrict non-academic use to church services and occasional community meetings.

Dorlin and Shielfoot Estates

The stately estate houses of the Loch Sunart and Loch Shiel areas are disappearing. First Shielbridge House was demolished, then Glencripesdale Castle and Dorlin House. The latter was built by Aeneous MacDonald, initially as a one-storey building in Georgian style.

Shielbridge House was one of the prominent landmarks of Ardnamurchan, commanding a view of Loch Shiel. It was built for Charles Rudd over a century ago. It was his favourite residence, as it was likewise the favourite residence of his successor Kenneth Clark. Mrs Holman, sister of Lord Trent, sold Shielbridge House to a Glasgow company. Owing to high taxation they decided to demolish it in 1951.

In 1855 Dorlin Estate was bought for £2,400 by James Hope Scott, a grandson of the second Earl of Hopeton. In 1847 he married Charlotte Mariot Jane, grand-daughter of Sir Walter Scott. It was through this marriage that James Hope acquired the additional name of Scott. Her highland home was Dorlin House until her death in 1858.

Hope Scott, as he was locally known, did much to improve the estate, constructing roads, improving houses and erecting a church and school at Mingarry. His second wife was Lady Victoria Alexandrina Fitzalan Howard whom he married in 1861. Queen Victoria was her god-mother. After this marriage Hope Scott had the three-storey house built at Dorlin, on a time and stuff agreement, by an Inverness firm. The foreman joiner, Mr John MacLellan, married and settled at Mingarry. The stone for the house was quarried just behind the house, but most of the other material came by boat to Salen pier on Loch Sunart.

Before the Roman Catholic church at Mingarry was built there was a Catholic church at Dorlin in which, it is said, two priests were buried. Hope Scott had the bodies lifted and reinterred at Eilean Fhianain. The building is still intact and used as a workshop today.

In 1871 Hope Scott sold the estate to Lord Howard of Glossop. He too was a benevolent landlord and Dorlin House saw many times of gaiety with frequent parties held during the fishing and shooting seasons. He died in 1924 and the property changed hands again twice, though the last owner never lived in it.

During the second world war Dorlin House was occupied for Commando training but then fell into disrepair and was eventually demolished.

Camus-Nan-Geall

In a field at the Bay of Camus-nan-Geall is a burial ground, Cladh Chiaran. The ruined outer wall and a rubble masonry inner structure are 18th century. Contemporary notes in the Ardslignish family bible indicate that the ground was used for burial of Roman Catholic members of the Campbell family of Ardslignish who resided at Camus-nan-Geall at that time. Carvings on the few surviving headstones within the ground further support that view.

A standing stone south-west of the burial ground was probably erected in the Bronze Age. Several motifs, carved in low-relief and including crosses and an animal, have been added since.

In 1905 two Fleetwood fishermen, crew members of a trawler anchored in Tobermory Bay, were drowned when their boat was swept out to sea while they were rowing from Tobermory pier to the trawler. Their bodies came ashore at Camus-nan-Geall and were interred outside the burial ground.

There is also a burial ground south-west of the farmhouse at Ardslignish. The site is marked 'Old Burrying Ground' on Bald's estate survey of 1806 but is not marked on Ordnance Survey maps. Local legend associates it with St Ciaran who is recorded as having died on

Camus·Nan·Geal

9 September 548 in Ireland. Within the enclosure lie the remains of a wall of significant thickness and about 30 feet long which may have been part of a building.

Near the burial ground stand the remnants of a chambered cairn. Though much material has been removed to construct nearby dwellings, identifiable sections of the structure, once roughly a semi-circle of about 30ft radius, are still visible.

Another ancient construction in the area is a stone fort close to the seaward end of the western arm of the bay. The remains, though limited, represent what was clearly a strongly-sited erection, having steep 50ft cliffs on three sides.

Ormsaigbeg

Ormsaigbeg is a small village just west of Kilchoan commanding a magnificent view of the Sound of Mull and Loch Sunart, with the hills of Mull and Morvern and Ben Hiant nestling in their waters.

Nearby is Sron Bheag, beyond which is a cave which is only accessible by sea and the entrance to which is partially obscured by a waterfall. it was the hiding place of a band of body-snatchers with whom another MacIain, MacGhiorr, was associated. Their boat was painted white on one side and black on the other. After an interval following an interment in the graveyard, they sailed the boat into Kilchoan Bay, uplifted the body and sailed away. Because of the two colours, positive identification of the boat was difficult.

The bodies were presumably transferred to Edinburgh and sold to Messrs Burke and Hare, who were notorious for their supply of bodies for research.

In 1906, about one mile west of Rubha Coilum, Ormsaigbeg, two local men drowned when their salmon-fishing skiff capsized. A third member of the crew managed to keep afloat with the aid of some flotsam until the mail boat, 'Staffa', inward bound from Coll and making for Kilchoan Bay, rescued him.

In the spring of 1909 two brothers and the young son of one of them were drowned on a passage between Tobermory and Kilchoan. Their sailing skiff was seen by people in Ormsaigbeg (where the brothers lived) from the time she appeared out of Tobermory Bay until she was abreast of the Red Rocks. There she disappeared in a heavy snow shower, and nothing more was seen of either the vessel or her crew.

Caisteal Dubh Nan Cliar

The translation of this name may be significant. The death of Angus, Lord of the Isles, at the hands of his minstrel at Ormsaigbeg has been noted earlier and the possibility has been mooted that this strong-point thus earned its name, the Black Castle of the Minstrels.

Expert opinion concedes that the age of the structure is uncertain, but it is tentatively placed in the 16th or 17th centuries. Angus was assassinated in 1490 so the link is a questionable one though not impossible.

The site of the Black Castle, above the foreshore of Kilchoan Bay, and its small size, suggest that it was an outpost of Mingary Castle, used possibly to protect the anchorages in the bay below.

Castle Tioram

Castle Tioram's ruins are at Dorlin. It was built in the 14th century and was the ancient stronghold of Clanranald. In 1644 it was occupied on behalf of Montrose by MacColla and the next year it was beseiged by Argyll. It is said to have been garrisoned by the Protectorate and to have been burned by its owner, Alan of Clanranald, when he led his clansmen off to join Mar's standard in 1715, in fear of being beseiged by the Campbells.

Ardnamurchan Lighthouse

The lighthouse was designed by Alan Stevenson in 1846 and was built by Robert Hume, a Gatehouse-of-Fleet contractor. The lighthouse became operational in 1849, at a total construction cost of £13,738. The stone used in construction is pink granite from the North Bay quarry in the Ross of Mull, the stones being shaped to provide for locking together.

the Lighthouse

The general design has been influenced by Egyptian architecture and this can be seen in the archways inside the houses, and those near the top of the tower. It is 114 feet high, and has a revolving light of some 27,000 candle-power which originally gave two flashes every 30 seconds.

Several of the original items of equipment in the lightroom remained until recent de-manning; they included a barometer by Adie & Son, Edinburgh, and a brass clock on wrought-iron brackets. The original lens mechanism also survived intact until the de-manning. The lightroom is reached through a doorway at the base and a flight of 140 steps built round a hollow central shaft.

Associated buildings erected to provide workshop and stabling facilities for the resident keepers stand nearby. A walled garden, and a sundial also by Adie and Son, are features of the setting.

The lighthouse is administered, like all the Scottish lighthouses, by the Northern Lighthouse Board which celebrated its Bicentenary in 1986.

To mark the occasion, Her Majesty the Queen expressed a wish to visit Ardnamurchan Lighthouse. On August 11, after some unfounded misgivings about her health, Her Majesty disembarked from the Royal Yacht 'Britannia' anchored off Mingary Pier. Accompanied by the newly-married Duke and Duchess of York and other members of the Royal Family, she was driven to the lighthouse. She climbed the steps to the lightroom "without pausing for breath".

Sadly, the day was to mark a watershed in the history of the lighthouse. By late autumn the process of modernisation in the form of automation began and a temporary light was installed.

All original furnishings – the clock, the barometer, the lenses, the clockwork mechanism which since 1928 lightkeepers climbed the flight of stairs to wind 'every hour and forty minutes' from sunset to sunrise – disappeared back to Edinburgh to be replaced by austere steel lockers containing computerised gadgetry monitored from Edinburgh.

The intensity of light, or lack of it, now activates the light, with a new characteristic of 2 flashes every 20 seconds. Similarly the density of fog or mist automatically switches on the foghorn, giving 2 blasts every 20 seconds.

Following de-manning, the redundant property at the site was sold and the Board has retained only the tower itself, the quarter-deck and the ex-Occasional Keeper's Cabin.

A report by the Lighthouse missionary dated 30 December 1857 says:

'I reached Ardnamurchan station on the morning of 2nd October and remained at it until the 13th. It is distant 5 miles from the parish church, there is a school 3 miles off but the Lightkeepers derive no advantage from it.

The Principal Keeper is married and has eight children. Their ages are respectively as follows:- a girl 14, boys of 12, 10, 8, 7, 4 and 3, and the youngest is an infant. The Assistant Keeper is also married and has three children, all of them quite young. The Principal Keeper during my visit was making arrangements for having 4 of his boys sent to the parish school. For this purpose he rented a house for them to live in with their grandmother in its immediate neighbourhood. This is an excellent arrangement as the parish schoolmaster is an excellent teacher. The two Lighthouse Keepers attend church pretty frequently during the summer and autumn months, but their wives and families very seldom enjoy this privilege.'

Those visits to lighthouses were carried out until shortly before the last war and were resumed a little over a decade ago by ministers from the Seamen's Mission, though de-manning has made them no longer necessary.

The parish schoolmaster referred to was John McCowan, who taught there from 1843-1874. He died on 4 January 1889 aged 90 and is buried in the old graveyard. His headstone was erected by the people of Kilchoan. Mr McCowan was also Registrar and Session Clerk.

The school was then in the part of the Kilchoan Hotel which is now the kitchen, and the ground westward from there to the corner of Pier Road was cultivated as the school croft. The new school and schoolhouse were built on the croft ground. In 1880 Mr A MacPherson succeeded Mr McCowan as teacher.

Population

The story of Ardnamurchan's population is one of fluctuation. That there were people on the peninsula long before the Roman invasion of 55BC is clear from the tangible clues they left about their way of life. These range from an early example of a beaker to show the presence of the Beaker people from the lower Rhine basin, to megalithic remains at various places.

Such races would have been represented by people counted in perhaps dozens, and, though figures for the centuries immediately following are unavailable, the total population in the first quarter of the eighteenth century was under a thousand. It rose from that to a peak of 3311 in 1831 and thereafter declined consistently, ruined buildings throughout the parish telling of townships and hamlets that were thriving in earlier times.

The decline was spread evenly over the three districts of Kilchoan, Acharacle and Strontian, until in 1951 the figure again dropped below the thousand, to 948. That figure was arrived at as follows:- Kilchoan, 287; Acharacle, 386; and Strontian, 275.

The nadir in 1971 was followed by a small increase ten years later. Exact breakdowns by settlement areas are no longer available since local government re-organisation in 1976, but regional council estimated figures for Ardnamurchan generally suggest that the population is again over one thousand and will continue at its present level for the immediate future at least.

The accompanying graph gives a vivid picture of the rise and fall in the population of Ardnamurchan from the beginning of the 18th century to the present. The level after 1981 has been extrapolated from local authority estimates.

Much of the decline is readily blamed on the clearances, though the following extract from the Inverness Courier for 11 October 1837, suggests the emigrants were not always penniless crofters driven by adversity to seek homes abroad.

'A large body of emigrants sailed from Tobermory, on the 27 September for New South Wales. The vessel was the "Brilliant" and its size and splendid fittings were greatly admired. The people to be conveyed by this vessel are decidedly the most valuable that have ever left the shores of Great Britain. They are of excellent moral character, and from their knowledge of agriculture and management of sheep and cattle, must prove a most valuable aquisition to a colony like New South Wales.

The Rev Mr MacPherson, of Tobermory, preached a farewell sermon before the party sailed. The total number of emigrants was 322, made up as follows:- From Ardnamurchan and Strontian 105; from Coll and Tiree 104; from Mull and Iona 56; from Morvern 25; and from Dunoon 28; there were two teachers and two surgeons.

A visitor from New South Wales presented as many of the party as he met with letters of introduction, and expressed himself highly gratified with the prospect of having so valuable an addition to the colony. A Government agent superintended the embarkation.'

The rise over recent decades must be attributed chiefly to the establishment of the many fish farms in the area and to their associated shore-bases. Tourism too has bought increased employment and may be expected to continue to do so as facilities, especially roads, improve. Other long-established industries including forestry continue to provide employment both directly and in down-stream spin-off operations.

Once the only road linked Salen pier with that at Ardtoe. There was no road between Salen and Strontian. Until relatively recently the chief means of transport consisted of the steamer, Clanranald II, which took passengers and cargo each day up to Loch Shiel to join the train at Glenfinnan. On Loch Sunart there was a twice-weekly sea service between Oban and Salen pier, and additional cargo boat sailings from Glasgow.

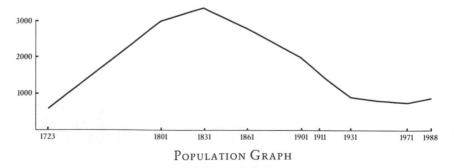

POPULATION GRAPH

The services were discontinued at the turn of the century and Salen pier became derelict though it has since been restored to use and today functions as a landing-place from fishing and pleasure vessels.

Only in the mid-'70s was electricity installed on the peninsula from Glenborrodale to Ormsaigbeg. Some houses before that had been served by generators installed by the householders themselves. A few years later the townships on the north coast had electricity brought to them.

Geology

In a booklet of this nature it is perhaps questionable that geology finds space. But the Ardnamurchan peninsula has a special, and internationally known, place in the 'annals' of geology which justifies at least outline coverage.

The Ardnamurchan landscape is the result of two major, yet vastly different, phases in geological history. The first was an outburst of volcanic activity, the second an Ice Age. Before the volcanicity the peninsula was part of an area of very ancient rocks which was overrun by sea, resulting in it being covered by sand, mud and limestone.

Fossils of extinct varieties of seashells (ammonites and grypheae [Devil's toe-nails]) can be seen near Mingary Castle and on the coast near Swordle in the limestones and shale. Through those beds some 60 million years ago lavas erupted, part of a phenomenon which occurred from the Giant's Causeway in Antrim to the south, through Ardnamurchan, to Skye and St Kilda to the north.

Lava flows of basalt, forming terrace-like features on the hillsides, can be seen at Ardslignish and across the water in Morvern and Mull. MacLean's Nose, south of Ben Hiant, displays spectacular cliffs of agglomerate (large and small blocks of rock of all shapes and type) filling the site of a former volcanic vent.

Of greatest interest to geologists however, who come from all over the world to see it, is the area surrounding Achnaha. Clearly seen on the road to Sanna (and particularly on aerial photographs) is a circular range of hills, up to 250 metres high, which surrounds a natural amphitheatre some 2-3 kilometres across. Its centre is one kilometre east of Achnaha.

Locally referred to as a crater, it is actually a rock stucture known as a ring-dyke, a solidified mass of liquid lava which formed in the circular chamber some 5km below a volcano long since removed by erosion. It is composed of a gabbro-type rock, similar to that forming the mountains of Rhum and the Cuillins of Skye and referred to by geologists as the

Great Eucrite.

Ardnamurchan's second most influential phase of geological development took place during the Ice Age, a period some 10,000 years ago when Scotland was covered by glaciers, sometimes thousands of metres thick. As they moved, rocks carried at the sides and bases of the glaciers removed the soil cover and also the existing rocks, scratching 'striae' in the latter and finally smoothing them into characteristic rounded outcrops. The direction of movement, to the WNW, can be ascertained by the directions of the striae and slopes of the outcrops and from the origins of some of the glacier-transported rocks deposited when the ice melted.

The ice tended to follow existing glens, deepening the floor and straightening the sides (e.g. Glen Tarbert) and in many cases creating the deep sea lochs of Scotland's west coast.

The weight of ice depressed the land surface. When the ice melted the land recovered, often rising more than the global sea-level and resulting in 'raised beaches' being seen today many metres inland around Scotland. At Kilchoan for example shingle and sea-shells are frequently found in excavations in the crofters' fields.

Sanna Bay is renowned for its white sands and dunes, both made up of broken-up sea-shell debris, washed and blown inland from the sea. The sands are 99.9% calcium carbonate, unlike common sea-sands which consist mainly of small grains of quartz.

Black streaks in the Ardnamurchan sands are made up of magnetite (a magnetic ore of iron) which has survived the disintegration of the other minerals of the gabbros of the area over the centuries since the Ice Age.

Wildlife

O primrose that growest
So pallid and sweet on the brae
In tender tufts blowing
In curly leaves flowing
The hardiest flower art thou
Sprung from the clay;
ALASDAIR MAC MAIGHSTIR ALASDAIR

The Ardnamurchan peninsula ranges from sea and shoreline to mountain and moorland. Though sometimes near-arctic, conditions generally are tempered by the Gulf Stream and the North Atlantic Drift. Together with the rich Sunart woodlands, this spectrum of geographic and climatic variation provides a diversity of conditions and habitat naturally encouraging a great variety of flora and fauna. It creates one of the finest and richest areas of natural history in Europe.

Wildcats and foxes are numerous as is the shy and secretive pine marten which is re-appearing after near-extinction. A healthy population of otters throughout the peninsula from shore to hill lochan feeds mainly on crabs and eels. Some fine herds of red deer can be seen throughout the year and in the woodlands are several small pockets of roe deer and of red squirrels.

The chequered skipper is a rare and beautiful butterfly now extinct in England and much of Scotland but still found in Ardnamurchan. Because of the pollution-free air, water and land there is an abundance of other butterflies and moths, and of insects including dragonflies and the notorious midge.

The native woodlands of Loch Sunart-side include oak, birch, ash, hazel, rowan, holly and a few alders. In those woods are resident sparrowhawks, and migrant willow- and wood-warblers sing all day in the spring. Sometimes seen too is the flash of the brightly-coloured redstart or a great spotted woodpecker. The full list of avian species to be seen on the peninsula is a long one.

There are many birds of prey ranging from Britain's smallest, the merlin, to the largest, the golden eagle. The forestry blocks, housing innumerable voles, have thus encouraged the influx of short-eared owls and hen harriers. Buzzards are common, often seen sitting on fences or telegraph poles.

One bird of prey which has been extinct in Scotland for almost 100 years is the sea eagle or erne. Resulting chiefly from a project on the Isle of Rhum aimed at re-introducing this largest of European eagles, there have been sporadic sightings of individual birds on the Ardnamurchan peninsula. The project has begun to bear fruit in recent years with young birds successfully fledged from eyries in remote corners of the western Highlands in most years since 1985. There are hopes that perhaps one day there will be a nest on Ardnamurchan.

The coast-line is home for many species of duck, among them eider, shellduck, mallard, and red-breasted merganser. Others seen there include oyster-catchers, curlews, herons and rock pipits. On the sea cliffs are shags and fulmars and luck sometimes allows an occasional glimpse of a peregrine falcon.

One of the most important features of the woods is the vast range of lichens, mosses and liverworts, indicating again the high level of atmospheric purity which makes this one of the richest parts of Europe for the group.

Flora too covers a broad spectrum of variety, including seapinks, campions, primroses, bluebells, English stonecrop, scabius, mountain thyme and many different species of orchid, to name only some of the more common plants. Less common species seen here are bog orchids, – Britain's smallest orchid – purple saxifrage, northern rock cress, bugle pyramidalis and the beautiful parnassus grass.

Two Ardnamurchan plants of North American origin are rare in Britain. They are pipewort – which is aquatic – and the orchid, Irish lady's tresses. The mystery of why they are found on the peninsula remains unsolved.

At sea there may be sightings of porpoises and dolphins, seals basking on the rocks, and, very occasionally, killer whales around Ardnamurchan point.

The area sometimes enjoys visits from rare species and the red kite – the American yellow-billed cuckoo – the clouded yellow butterfly, and a school of 150 pilot whales have all been seen in past years, helping to maintain the peninsula's reputation for its wealth of opportunity for serious study or for satisfying mere curiosity.

> Now soft the minutes fall! Now like the snow,
> Invader with no colours and no drum,
> drifting, drifting, drifting, filling up
> our lives with quiet the eider seconds come.
>
> Time creeps and silence creeps whether we sit
> and watch the burial of the world we know
> or strap ourselves into our disbelief
> and down the thickening street unsteady go.
>
> ALASDAIR MACLEAN

4

ORIGINS OF SOME OF
THE GAELIC PLACE-NAMES OF THE PENINISULA

Picts and Druids, Danish kings and pirates, Irish saints, wandering princes and Lords of the Isles have all made contributions to our present-day names. We may study and we may speculate but to be dogmatic would be dangerous as in many of the names there are 'options'. Thanks to the Ordnance Survey mapmakers many names have been recorded which would otherwise have been forever lost and despite the fact that most of those engaged in preparing the maps would be non-Gaelic-speakers and dependent on phonetic renderings, the results, with one or two exceptions, have been very correctly recorded.

Townships or settlements

Acarsaid G. *Acairseid* A harbour or anchorage.

Achateny G. *Acha' Teine* The field of fire.

Achnaha G. *Acha' na h-ath* The field of the ford. (Ath can mean a ford or a kiln. Here the ford is that on the large stream Allt uamha na muice, the burn of the cave of the pig).

Achosnich G. *Ach' osnaich* The field of the sighing, or gusts of, wind.

Acharacle G. *Ath'-Tharracail* Torquil's ford. The English version has been misspelt and should be Aharacle. The ford is on the river Shiel. Legend tells that Torquil was leading the Norse force pursued by Somerled which made a stand by the river, just below Acharacle Manse and was slain there.

Ardslignish G. *Aird Sleiginnis* The height of the meadow abounding in shells. The two islands off Ardslignish are An-t-sleigneach bheag and An-t-sleigeach mhor.

Ardtoe G. *Airdto* A hybrid of the Gaelic aird, a height, and Norse haugr or howe, a burial place.

Arivegaig G. *Airidh-Bheagaig* The sheiling of the little bay.

Braehouse G. *Bra' h-abhasa* A difficult one, but where we think the Ordnance Survey got it wrong. Close by there is a little stream called an-t-abhsadh, erratic or going off at a tangent, so, head of the stream An-tAbhsadh.

Branault G. *Braigh nan allt* The brae or head of the streams.

Buarblaig G. *Buarbalaig* Probably from buar, cattle or cattle-fold, baile, a farm, and aig, a bay. It has also been suggested that it might be from the Norse, borg+ bol+ vik = fort+ steading+ bay. It might also be associated with the Firbolg, the early British Belgae who settled in Ireland and made frequent raids to Scotland.

Caim G. *A'Chaim* The bend. Wrongly listed on OS maps as Camphouse. Called A'Chaim because of the bend in the Allt Coire Mhuillin at that particular place.

Camusinas G. *Camus Aonghais* Angus's bay.

Camus Ban G. *Camus ban* White bay.

Camus nan Geall Gaelic spelling could be 1) *Camus A'Gheall*, the bay of promise or of success or 2) *Camus an Gall*, the bay of the stranger or 3) *Camus nan Gall*, the bay of the stangers or foreigners or 4) *Camus nan Geall*, the bay of the promises or wagers or vows, as taken by monks or 5) *Camus nan Ceall*, bay of cells or churches. The choice is left to the reader!

Camus fern G. *Camus fearna* Bay of the alders

Camus a'choirc The bay of corn or the knife

Coiremhuillin G. *Coire mhuilinn* The corrie of the mill

Corrachary G. *Corrach-airigh* The steep shieling (not on the map – a former settlement beyond Grigadale).

Culorne G. *Cuil Eadhrain* Corner of Eadhran. This place is close to Cladh Chatain and Eadhran (Erin) was an Irish poet.

Cuiloven G. *Cuil eoghainn* Hugh's corner (one at Achosnich and one behind Ben Hiant).

Eigneig G. *Eigneig* Oak bay. Norse Eik, oak, and Vik, bay.

Grigadale G. *Girgeadal* Field of gravel. Norse grjot, dalr, dale.

Glenborrodale G. *Gleann Borrodail* Some controversy exists as to this origin. Most likely from norse Borg, a fort, and dalr, dale.

Glendrian G. *Gleann an Draighinn* The glen of the thorn bushes.

Goirtean Eorna G. *Goirtean Eorna* The cornfield of barley.

Glenmore G. *An gleann mor* The big glen.

Glenbeg G. *An gleann beag* The small glen.

Gobshellach G. *An Gob-seileach* The point of the willows, or the mouth or point of the river Shiel.

Inbhir Luachrach G. *Inbhir Luachrach* The reeded estuary. Once a settlement between Ru' Dubh and Sanna where Brathair nam Allt flows into the sea. The ruins are on the Sanna side of the river.

Innis nam Feorag G. *Innis nan feorag* The valley of the squirrels.

Kilchoan G. *Cille Chomhain*, earlier *Cille Chothain*, later spelling *Cille Chomhghain*. Church dedicated to St Coan or St Comgan or St Comhghan. He was patron saint of the old Glengarry family.

Kentra G. *Ceanntraigh* Head of the beach.

Laga G. *Laga* A hollow. Norse lagr and ey, island.

Mingary G. *Mionghairidh* Presents a poser. It has been translated as Mioghairidh – the whey sheiling, and as the great garth from Mikinn, great, and gard, garth. The name is found in Mull, Moidart and Benbecula and may simply mean middle garden, from Meadhon, middle, and garadh, a garden.

Ockle G. *Ochdal* Early translations given as Pictish as in Uchel meaning high, as used for example in the Ochil Hills, Ochiltree and the Oykell river. Dr Gillies gives it Norse origin, Ok, a yoke and dalr, a dale. The local traditional translation Ochd, eight, and dail, a field, seems to be the simplest as apparently Ockle was originally divided into eight shares.

Ormsaig G. *Ormsaighheag* and *Ormsaigmhor* Has been translated as from Norse orme, a serpent and vik, a bay, giving serpent bay. Other possibilities put forward: One Viking chief, Horm Storolfson, led his men down the west coast conquering as he went. He was killed off Anglesey in 856 AD. His name has been given to the promontory Great Orme's Head and to Ormskirk in Lancashire and to Ormsary (Orm's airhigh) near Lochgilphead so perhaps Ormsaig is Orm's mooring or anchorage.

Plocaig G. *Plocaig* Ploc, a lump, and vik, a bay, The ploc is probably the huge square-cut promontory called A'Charraig, a sea rock or shore line jutting into the sea. (Sadly, the place Carraig is now regularly referred to as The Cat's Face by recent incomers because of markings on the rock face.)

Portuairk G. *spelling controversial.* Some people pronounce this township *Port Uairce* as did the population census of 1891. This would come from the aspirated form of suairce meaning pleasant, an unlikely meaning in an area where there are numerous 'pleasant ports' and the Gaels were not prone to using romantic names to describe places. The second pronounciation is *Port Uaraig* or *Port Uaric*, which appears in some of the Session Books. This would come from the personal name Ulrig, a Norse warrior who made his way down the western seaboard. The name Ulrig is still used by the Kennedy clan who call themselves Clannuaric after a chief called Ulric Kennedy who settled in Lochaber.

Salen G. *Sailean* Salty Creek. There are several Salens on the west coast and they invariably apply to a heel-shaped bay of salt water. In Sunartside are Sailean an Eorna, Salen of the barley, Sailean nan Cuileag, Salen of the flies (or midges) and Sailean-Sunart which is the full name for what is now Salen village. The inner reach of Kilchoan bay used to be called Sailean Chille-Chothain.

Sanna G. *Sana* Probably from the Norse Sandr, sand, and ey, island. It probably took its name as a township, after the clearances, from the island Eilean Shana. Other places around are Meall Shana, the hill or mound of Sanna, Rudha Shana, Sanna Point, and Bealach Shana, the gap between Sanna and Achosnich. Note: The original may have been spelt with a T, Tana, meaning neat or shelved, hence Eilean Thana, Rudha Thana etc.

Skinid G. *Sginid* This is probably from the Norse skith, a tablet or flat surface, and inid, a place. (There is another Skjinid in Sutherland and in Caithness a parish called Skinnet).

Swordle G. *Suardail* A grassy field.

Tarbert G. *Tairbeart* From tar, across, and bear, carry – an isthmus.

Tomachrochair G. *Tom A'Chrochaire* The hangman's knoll.

The names of the hills and mountains, lochs and tarns, points, waterfalls and bays are mostly straightforward and almost exclusively Gaelic. Although of immense interest, space does not permit the inclusion of all of them. Some of the more unusual or those unmapped or having a story are worth mentioning.

Rudha Gead Na Brathan Point of the ridge of the quern stones or handmill stones, which supplied millstones for the whole area.

Lag A'Choire Hollow of the kettle. A still was in use here for the distilling of whisky, using the water from the burn Alt Fheahrghais (Fergus's burn). One particular part in the upper reaches of Lag A'Choire has a place which has traditionally been called Brathleis Domhnaill Chaimbeul (the 'wort' or 'still' of Donald Campbell).

Eas A'Ghille Luideanach The waterfall of the ragged boy, on the Sanna road not far from the turn-off. It is said that a tinker's child fell down the waterfall and was drowned and that on a certain day each year the sound of wailing is heard because of the tragedy.

Car na Pheursa The bend of the signal flag. On the Ormsaigmore side of the road near Sanna turn-off. One of the points where the signal was hoisted when word was passed that the gauger was in the area, (looking for the illicit dram).

Beinn nan Codhan The hill of the coffins.

Eilean nan Gillean The island of the boys. Gillean na sronne - boys of the point. Four brothers had gone to visit friends at Dorlin across Loch Sunart and all four were drowned and their bodies found on this island.

Meall an Tarmachain Hump or hill of the ptarmigan. Reminiscent of the days when this member of the grouse family was plentiful on the high mountain-tops.

Lochan na Crannaig The pulpit loch, (or loch na Crannog, loch of the crannog, a lake dwelling).

Loch Mudle G. *Loch Mudail* Possibly from the Norse modr, muddy, and dalr, dale.

Loch nan Sioman Loch of the heather ropes.

Loch Moidart G. *Loch Muideart* From modr, muddy, and fjord, a ford or sea loch.

Loch Sunart G. *Suaineart* Swynaort (1392) Sweyn's ford. Sweyn was a Danish king, the father of Canute of British history. He overcame Norway about 1000 AD, England some years later and between times the whole of the west of Scotland.

Rudha Murchanach Ardnamurchan Point.

Eilean nan Seachd Seisrichean Island of the seven teams (of horses for ploughing).

Morvern G. *Mur-Bhearna* The sea gap, Loch Sunart being the gap.

Cladh Chiaran The grave of St Kiaran, a bishop and schoolfellow of St Columba. After labouring in Cornwall, where he is known as St Piran, he came to the west of Scotland and worked for many years at Campbeltown (Ceann-loch-cille-chiaran). Said to have died on 9 September 548.

Rudha Champ an Righ Apparently when James IV visited Mingary Castle he combined business with pleasure by arranging to go boar hunting on the island of Orasa. He established his camp at this point from whence came the name, point of the king's camp.